D0182757

ALL IN THE
MIND

ALL IN THE
MIND

Psychology in Action

Edited by
John Nicholson and Martin Lucas

THAMES METHUEN

This book was devised and produced by
Multimedia Publications (UK) Limited in
association with Thames Television

Editor Caroline Morrow Brown
Associate Editors Janet Law and Susana Raby
Design John Strange
Picture Research Paul Snelgrove

Copyright © 1984 Multimedia Publications
(UK) Ltd

First published in Great Britain 1984 by
Methuen London Ltd, 11 New Fetter Lane,
London EC4P 4EE

in association with Thames Television
International Ltd, 149 Tottenham Court Road,
London W1P 9LL

British Library Cataloguing in Publication Data
All in the mind.
1. Psychology
I. Nicholson, John II. Lucas, Martin
150 BF121

ISBN 0 423 00920 6
ISBN 0 423 00930 3 Pbk

This title is available in both hardback and paperback
editions. The book is sold subject to the condition that
it shall not, by way of trade or otherwise, be lent,
re-sold, hired out or otherwise circulated without the
publisher's and the copyright holder's prior consent in
any form of binding or cover other than that in which it
is published and without a similar condition including
this condition being imposed on the subsequent
purchaser.

Typeset by Text Filmsetters Ltd, Orpington, UK.
Printed in Spain by Mateu Cromo Artes
Graficas SA.

Contents

The attractive advertising poster, the tempting shop display, the patter of the street market stallholder – all use psychological devices to persuade us to spend more.

WHAT IS PSYCHOLOGY? 1

Over the last one hundred years, many of the ideas and theories of professional psychologists have been absorbed into everyday thinking. They have also contributed to social policy-making, and now influence a whole variety of public activities, from the way violent criminals are treated to the design of motor car seats. This influence is even reflected in the way we speak. When we talk of 'conditioning' or of our 'IQ', when we say we are 'extravert' or 'introvert', or complain about 'stress' or 'subliminal advertising', we are using just a few of the host of psychological terms that have been drawn into our everyday language, reflecting the influence of psychology on our thinking.

Despite this widespread infiltration of psychological terms and ideas, many people are still confused about what psychology actually is and how it is done. Others doubt that the results of psychological research can be of any real value in their own lives. Yet others worry that psychology will become *too* effective, fearing that if psychologists ever manage to unravel the basic determinants of our behaviour and mental processes, it will leave us helpless puppets, easily manipulated and denied any real choice about how to behave.

In *All in the Mind*, we show that psychologists *can* provide useful and interesting answers to many of the questions that we ask about ourselves, and that these answers offer us the possibility of a *greater* freedom and responsibility – not less. We have made a selection from contemporary research which shows what kind of things

Thames Television's All in the Mind, *which formed the basis for this book, was produced and directed by Martin Lucas (above) and written and presented by John Nicholson (below), lecturer in psychology at Bedford College, London.*

psychologists actually do and how they go about it. Our selection is not made at random, however. We have chosen to look at what psychologists say about areas of human behaviour that are of direct concern to everyone: friendships and social relationships, intellectual development, fears and anxieties, for example. We also look at how psychological research is applied to important public issues, like the sources of criminal behaviour and how the working environment affects how happy and healthy we feel. Finally, we draw all these strands together to look at how psychology can help us to increase the possibilities for growth and change in our own lives.

As you read this book it will become clear to you that, far from reducing us all to mere puppets, the scientific study of behaviour reveals that each one of us is more complex and fascinating than we could ever have believed, and that the possibilities for our development, both individually and socially, are even greater than we might have hoped.

Psychology, psychiatry and psychoanalysis

A great deal of confusion exists about how psychology differs from psychiatry and psychoanalysis, yet the distinction is very clear-cut.

Psychiatry is a branch of medicine devoted to the treatment of mental illnesses and other disorders in which psychological factors are prominent. It is a medical speciality just like gynaecology or rheumatology, and every psychiatrist undergoes a conventional medical training before specializing in psychiatry. Psychologists, in contrast, are not required to study medicine, and most of psychology is concerned with the behaviour of normal rather than mentally disordered people. But some psychologists, called clinical psychologists, also specialize in the treatment of mental illness. In Britain a significant number of psychologists are employed as clinical psychologists in the National Health Service. The methods of treatment used by clinical psychologists tend to differ from those used by psychiatrists: only psychiatrists use physical methods of treatment such as drugs and ECT (electro-convulsive therapy, or shock treatment).

Psychoanalysis is a theory of mental structure and function and an associated method of treatment based on the writings of the Viennese physician, Sigmund Freud. Freud laid great emphasis on the role of the unconscious, and the main techniques of psychoanalysis

reflect this emphasis. *Free association* is a technique in which the person being analysed is encouraged to speak whatever enters his or her mind, without hesitation or censorship, with the aim of uncovering unconscious motives and conflicts. Dream analysis is based on free association, and is claimed to throw light on the symbolic meaning of the patient's dreams. A third technique focuses on the interpretation of *parapraxes* or, as they are popularly known, *Freudian slips*. Finally there is the technique of *transference* in which the therapeutic relationship is used to help the patient re-live past relationships with significant people in his or her life. A full analysis involves two or more sessions per week over a period of several years.

Most psychoanalysts are not formally trained in psychology or psychiatry. Some psychologists and psychiatrists, however, do go on to become psychoanalysts, and some who do not become fully fledged psychoanalysts none the less adopt a somewhat psychoanalytic approach to treatment. Most psychologists in Britain, however, have reservations about the value of psychoanalysis.

The symbolism of dreams as expounded by Freud and Jung is reflected in the work of modern artists such as Paul Nash, Paul Klee and René Magritte. Above: Nash's Landscape from a Dream.

An experimental laboratory with an electroencephalogram which records electrical activity in the brain.

Science and psychology

Almost all of us consider ourselves to be amateur psychologists. We all have our theories and intuitions about how children ought to be brought up or how criminals should be treated, and we all believe we have a pretty fair idea about what motivates other people, how to tell what they are really thinking and so on. However, these common-sense theories often reveal more about us than about the people we are trying to understand. They reflect the various influences that happen to have touched our lives and our own particular preferences and peculiarities. Many of us are reluctant to put our home-grown theories to a real test.

This is what distinguishes professional psychologists from the rest of us; they try not to make any observations about human or animal behaviour unless these observations have been tested by rigorous experiments. Similarly, the various theories which psychologists propose in order to make sense of the results of their experiments are abandoned if new data contradict them. In a real sense, the only purpose of a proper scientific experiment is to disprove, or at least show the inadequacy of, an existing theory. This is the only means by which psychologists can be at all confident that they are accumulating real and worthwhile insights, and it is quite different from the hit-or-miss conjecture which most of us use to come up with our favourite theories of human behaviour.

Experiments are also made in natural surroundings. Here the psychologist is testing the child's responses by playing games with him.

The key to real science lies in its method. Scientists come to an idea, a hypothesis. This is drawn from previously observed facts, but goes beyond the facts, and from it they should be able to make a prediction. As experimenters, they then have to devise or find a situation in which they can test their predictions. This doesn't have to be a laboratory, it can be anywhere or with any subject, as long as they can be sure that what they observe really is following or denying their predictions and isn't just an accidental result. Modern psychology experiments therefore depend heavily on carefully tested measuring devices and on sophisticated statistical analysis. Statistics are vital in psychological research, since all individual measurements have to be checked against the normal spread of results which might have occurred by chance. Statistical analysis is also needed to check that what's apparently true for a small group of subjects can be extended to observations about the larger population from which they came.

One weakness in this scientific approach is that progress is often made only by a series of small, apparently insignificant gains in information. Sometimes the result of an experiment merely seems to confirm what most people would have guessed at anyway. But psychologists believe that there is real value in scientifically establishing things that were previously simply popular wisdom. Although it's true that a good deal of the psychological information accumulated so far does not present us with radical surprises, psychologists have shown that many of our common-sense notions about human psychology completely fail to do justice to the complex processes which underlie even the most apparently simple behaviour.

Can psychology surprise us?

In his book *What is Psychology?*, psychologist Andrew Colman lists twenty such psychological 'surprises'. Examples are presented by him in the form of self-assessment quizzes, and it seems that people who have not studied psychology tend to get most, if not all, of the answers wrong. This first example is taken from a famous experiment in child development, which parents can easily repeat with their children at home. A row of, say, eight egg cups, each one containing an egg, is placed in front of a child, who is asked to confirm that the number of egg cups is the same as the number of eggs, which he or she will do. The child is then invited to watch while the eggs are removed one by one from the egg cups and placed together in a row that is slightly shorter than the row of egg cups. The child is then asked whether there are more eggs than egg cups, or more egg cups than eggs, or just the same.

It is difficult for a non-psychologist to predict how a particular child will respond to this problem, or to give a coherent explanation of the child's behaviour. In fact, if you do this experiment with children under about six and a half years of age, you will probably find that they think that there are now more egg cups than eggs. It seems that these young children focus on the relative length of the rows without taking into account the density of the rows. You might expect that a child who could count would give the right answer to the egg problem, but this is not necessarily so. Children who can say one, two, three and so on will count the eggs in the egg cups correctly, but will still say that somehow there are more egg cups than there are eggs. In other words, they have learned to count, but have yet to grasp the abstract concept of number.

This is a far from obvious result which may have important implications for education. A recent survey of 1714 children in Britain showed that only about one fifth of four- to five-year-olds give the right answer to this problem, whereas about four-fifths of the seven- to eight-year-olds were able to do it.

There are difficulties about interpreting this sort of experiment, which we touch on in Chapter 3. And before you smile at the intellectual naivety of young children, you should know that psychologists have discovered a very similar sort of failure of understanding in adults. This type of thing can be demonstrated by filling several equal-sized tin cans with varying amounts of a heavy material and preparing a larger can – say, double the volume of the small cans – so that its true weight exactly matches that of one of the small cans. Let us call the large can brand X, and the small cans brand A, brand B and so on. Adults, when invited to lift the cans and to guess which of the small cans is the same weight as the large ones, will almost invariably choose one that is really much lighter than the large brand X can. If, for example, brand X weighs three hundred grams, and the smaller cans (brands A, B, C, D and E) weigh one hundred, one hundred and fifty, two hundred, two hundred and fifty and three hundred grams respectively, most people will choose brand B or brand C as equal to brand X. Only about one person in fifty will correctly choose brand E. In other words, the error is of the order of about one third to one half!

This illusion is extremely powerful and persistent – even when the cans are weighed on a pair of scales in front of the subject. People shopping in supermarkets frequently succumb to the illusion. If they habitually compare the weights of different-sized packages by hand, they almost invariably make wildly inaccurate judgements.

A very different 'surprising finding' comes from the field of social psychology. It is widely believed that decisions made by committees are more cautious, more conservative and less extreme than those taken by individuals. However, experiments by social psychologists show that exactly the reverse is the case! It is group decisions which tend to be more extreme. During the course of a group discussion, the views of most group members tend to polarize in the direction of dominant group opinion. This is called *the group polarisation phenomenon*. Suppose that a group of six people is presented with the summary of a court case in which a man is convicted of raping a young woman. Before discussing the case, the group members are asked for their individual opinions on the proper severity of the sentence the rapist should receive. The options from which they must choose run from a warning right through to a very severe sentence. Even when the initial individual opinions range from a light sentence through to a very severe sentence, if the group

The process of group decision-making is brilliantly portrayed in Sidney Lumet's film Twelve Angry Men. Here Henry Fonda remains mute while the rest of the jury vote for a quick verdict of guilty.

is then invited to discuss the case until it has agreed upon a unanimous decision, the most likely final decision will be a very severe sentence. To be precise, the group decision is more likely to be more extreme toward the severe end of the scale than the average of the individual pre-discussion decisions.

This kind of effect applies across a wide range of group decisions. There seem to be several reasons for it, but the most important one is our dependency on social comparison. Apparently in a group discussion, cultural values become emphasized. Everyone likes to think of themselves as being, in this particular example, anti-rape, this being the predominant attitude in all but the most macho groups in our culture. When the discussion begins, however, several group members will discover that others have made individual decisions on the sentence which are even more severe than their own. These people now feel under pressure to show themselves and the other members of the group that they properly represent the cultural attitude, and that they are at least as anti-rape as the next person. So they revise their opinions in the direction of the severe sentence group. This tendency clearly undermines the whole principle of decision-making by committees so it is fortunate that psychology has a remedy for it.

This phenomenon has obvious and important implications for group decisions of all kinds, and it is often important to guard against group polarization. Here is how to do it. Before any important group discussion begins, get everyone involved to write down what they think the outcome of the discussion ought to be. *They must not reveal these initial positions until after the discussion is finished*. Instead, use them to check that the sum of the individuals' initial preferences has not been overruled by the group acting as a whole. If it has, find out why. Has one member of the group revealed an important new piece of information, for example? The crucial final check is that the decision about to be made is one that every member of the group is prepared to justify – *even if they do not agree with it*.

Examples like these give us some idea of the vast range of interests in modern psychology. Psychologists are currently carrying out research into almost every aspect of human behaviour, from the computer modelling of individual brain cells to the effects of town planning on human sociability and happiness. What unifies all these activities is the belief that it is possible to unravel complex and subtle behaviour, and discover the logical processes which must underlie it, through systematic scientific research. And this is a belief inherited from the first efforts of the very earliest scientific psychologists.

The beginnings of modern psychology
The word psychology had already come into the English language towards the end of the seventeenth century. Its Greek roots are the words *psyche* and *logos*. In Greek mythology, *Psyche* (usually depicted as a beautiful young woman with butterfly wings) is the personification of the human soul. In fact, the word psyche originally meant breath, but its meaning was gradually extended to include spirit or soul, because it was assumed that breath is evidence of life and therefore of the soul's presence in the body. Finally, it was extended to mean mind, the modern equivalent of soul. *Logos* originally meant 'word' and its meaning was later extended to include discourse or study. Thus, the literal meaning of psychology was the study of mind.

However, psychology is usually said to have begun as a scientific discipline in it own right when the German philosopher Wundt set up his experimental psychology laboratories in Leipzig in 1879. Wundt and his associates carried out experiments quite different from those performed by modern psychologists and for quite different reasons. They were actually philosophers of the human mind who were enormously impressed by the results of the scientific method as it was applied by nineteenth-century scientists and engineers. Ingenious inventors had shown that it was possible to build a whole range of devices, from the camera to the pianola, which could carry out functions previously assumed to be reserved for skilled human beings and creative human thought. Great strides were also being made as scientists became more specialized in their understanding of the natural world. Biologists, particularly, were collecting more and more data, specimens and fossils, which confirmed Darwin's radical insight into the evolutionary links between all living creatures.

In such a heady atmosphere, it is not surprising that Wundt and his associates could see no reason why the same kind of scientific approach should not be applied to

Wilhelm Wundt
(centre), founder of the first
psychological laboratory, in
Leipzig.

the study of the mind. By carefully observing and analysing their own thinking, a method that they called scientific introspection, they set out to discover the basic laws of the mind. They spent thousands of hours carefully recording and classifying the products of their own consciousness in an effort to establish what they believed to be the first scientific psychology.

What distinguished these new psychologists from those who had gone before them was that, instead of merely speculating, they attempted to carry out experiments to validate their ideas. The introspectionist psychologists and their followers faithfully observed their own ruminations well into the early twentieth century. Despite the primitiveness of their methods, they made some valuable observations which remain useful to psychologists even now, particularly about some of the basic elements of human perception. For example, they established that humans can respond to stimuli set at intensities or durations just below their conscious awareness (subliminal perception) and they investigated optical illusions and the curious ways in which the human mind will organize random arrangements of dots and lines so that they are seen as meaningful whole figures set against a background. However, what is most important about their early work is that they moved psychology from a preoccupation with profound but unanswerable questions to practical attempts to deal with answerable ones. In this sense they are the true founders of modern scientific psychology.

By the first years of the twentieth century, the work of

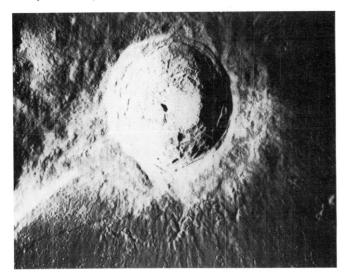

An optical illusion: is this a hill or a crater? It is, in fact, a picture of a crater on the moon's surface taken from a lunar orbiter.

the introspectionists was successful enough for several university departments to be set up in Britain, mainland Europe and the USA. An important influence came from animal studies, when the Russian psychologist Ivan Pavlov (1849-1936) proposed that he had discovered one of the fundamental building bricks of learning – the nervous link between a stimulus in the environment and an animal's response. He had been studying digestion, specifically the production of saliva in dogs, when he noticed that the dogs salivated not only when they were actually presented with food, but when they heard or saw any of the usual laboratory activity associated with the food. Pavlov realized that repeated association of the artificial laboratory sights and sounds with the presentation of the food had established some kind of link with the dogs' natural response. Even more important, he realized that he had been presented with a reliable means by which he could precisely control and

B.F. Skinner, born 1904, one of the best known and most controversial psychologists of our time.

measure the effect of a repeated stimulus on a dog's learned response. He could measure, for example, how many joint presentations of the sound of a bell and food were necessary before the dog salivated to the bell alone. He could measure how much saliva was produced and how quickly the response fell away, and most important of all, he could get the same predictable results again and again. Pavlov called this *conditioning*, and came to believe, as many psychologists still do, that he must be measuring one of the most basic learning processes, not only in animals but in human beings. Many psychologists were impressed by the real scientific objectivity of techniques like these, particularly compared to the often vague results of the earlier introspectionist efforts.

The most radical movement against the traditional introspective method was founded by John Watson, (1878-1958) in 1912, and he called it *behaviourism*. Watson decided that introspection of the mind as a scientific method got nowhere and was, in any case, founded on fallacy. How can you be scientific, he argued, about something that can't be seen, measured or controlled? We may know about our own mental experience, but we can never have direct knowledge of anyone else's and we can't even guess at the mental experience of other species. Behaviourists decided that they would only allow themselves to observe the objective facts of behaviour. They would ask no questions about what might or might not be going on in someone's head, but only about the circumstances in which their behaviour changed. Some behaviourists, notably the Harvard University professor, B.F. Skinner, went even further. Skinner came to believe, and still does, that all behaviour, both animal and human, is directed from the environment around us, not from within. Skinner decided that for all intents and purposes there was no such thing as mind at all.

At first sight, the behaviourists' radical approach seems austere and unrewarding, but it has had several valuable effects on psychology. The behaviourists would only accept the objective results of precise experiments which would bring about predicted and controlled changes in behaviour. If the psychologists who were still interested in mental processes wanted to challenge these theories, they had to become highly sophisticated in devising publicly observable experiments with clearly repeatable results. Psychology began to steer itself further and further away from vague theorizing, becoming increasingly concerned with effective experimental methods and the statistical analyses of results. Nevertheless, a great many psychologists continued to believe that it was possible to study thinking and feeling and yet to remain scientists: the behaviourist revolution was only partially successful.

As the twentieth century progressed, behaviourism's most dedicated followers confined their studies to relatively simple animals like rats or cats, using special apparatus like the Skinner box, in which an animal can gain a reward or avoid punishment as it learns to press a lever. They hoped to build up a detailed picture of the basic units of behaviour, particularly from the study of learning, and this experimental tradition is still influential, both in Britain and America. A substantial number of experimental psychologists, however, took a more reserved view. They accepted the necessity of working in carefully controlled laboratories. They used strict procedures and objective measures of behaviour change, but they were reluctant to accept that their human subjects' own reports on their thoughts and feelings could be of no value. A classic example of the validity of their reservations is a common experiment in which people are asked to make a response – say, pressing a button – as soon as they receive a signal. It is well known that the time it takes them to respond to the signal, the reaction time, varies with all sorts of factors. One major influence is the person's own attention. If they concentrate on the *response* they are going to make, their reaction time is quicker than if they concentrate on the *signal*. You can only find this out, however, if you ask them to introspect and consider their own thinking.

Another large group of psychologists accepted that there was a need for scientific rigour in their studies, but didn't want to work in the artificial confines of laboratories at all. They wanted to study individuals in groups and in real-life situations. They wanted to try and understand the effects of normal influences in people's lives, like the way their parents had reared them, or their conditions of work. It became clear that a useful psychology would not come exclusively from the study of human mental processes or animal behaviour, according to some particular technical theory. Instead it would come from the careful application of increasingly sophisticated scientific methods to any question about the behaviour of living creatures, whether individuals or groups, healthy or abnormal. And so, there is still no universally accepted definition of psychology. But the

Skinner designed a special box in which to investigate the effects of rewards and punishments on operant behaviour in animals such as rats, cats or pigeons.

best rough and ready definition ought to include both mental experience and behaviour. Mental experiences can be divided into two main classes: *cognition*, that is, thinking and perceiving, and *emotion*, that is, feeling.

There is no one central and unified conception which ties together all the results and observations of psychologists. This makes psychology rather different from disciplines such as physics or chemistry, where, at a given time, most orthodox practitioners will subscribe to one unifying general theory. They use this to guide them in deciding what are useful problems to solve, what kinds of information are relevant and what to make of their results. This general theory will change over the years, sometimes dramatically, as new information becomes available. One effect of this difference is that psychologists have felt free not only to develop their own theories to guide their work, but to borrow freely from other disciplines over the years. Thus, psychologists have taken concepts from chemistry, electronics, communications, engineering, molecular biology and, most recently, computer science.

Different approaches to psychology

One useful way to understand the division of effort in psychology is to look at the kind of processes which different psychologists study. One large group of psychologists confine their studies entirely to investigation of the physiological processes which underlie the behaviour and mental functioning of individuals. The success of this kind of research largely depends upon the sophistication of the techniques and measuring equipment available. For example, since the 1930s, a great deal of information about the activity of the human brain has been gained by studying the electro-encephalogram (EEG) or brain wave patterns of people who are in different states of arousal, under the influence of various drugs, or attempting to carry out various mental tasks. Physiological psychology took a great step forward in the early 1960s, when psychologists developed surgical techniques to implant fine electrodes into an animal's brain which could detect the activity of tiny groups of brain cells and relate this activity to changes in the environment. The ethics of this kind of surgical intervention into an animal's behaviour are still hotly debated, but it has enabled psychologists to find out a great deal about the brain mechanisms which we share with other animals.

For example, using surgery and conditioning

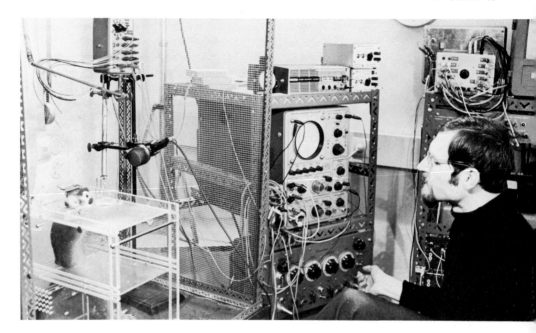

techniques with rats, Jeffrey Gray, Professor of Psychology at the Institute of Psychiatry in London, has studied the brain processes underlying anxious behaviour. Gray believes that inherited variations in this and other basic mechanisms have a profound effect on human personality and considerable implications not only for activities like child rearing and teaching, but also for the treatment of emotional disturbance. Thus he claims that people who have inherited an 'anxious' nervous system will learn most efficiently when threatened with punishment and are therefore more likely to develop maladapted or neurotic behaviour. From this perspective, the correct treatment of neurosis is not long hours of Freudian analysis, but a short, active programme where a person can simply unlearn their neurotic responses and learn new ones. British psychologists have been influential in developing *behaviour therapy*, an approach discussed and exemplified in Chapters 7 and 8.

Other psychologists study how we change over time: one crucial influence on all our behaviour is our age and our stage of development. There is now a great deal of information on how our social and intellectual abilities change as we mature, and it looks increasingly encouraging. Recently, psychologists have developed ingenious techniques for recording minute changes in the behaviour of tiny babies, which give an objective indication of their awareness of the world around them.

Electrical stimulation of the squirrel monkey's brain produces a particular response which can be measured and studied.

21

If a baby shows a consistent preference for looking at one of two objects presented to it, we know that it can discriminate between them. Similarly, babies prefer to look at novel stimuli than at familiar ones. Using these kinds of techniques, it is now well established that babies have a far more subtle and detailed awareness of what is going on around them than we had previously assumed (see Chapter 3). For example, one recent study has found that even one-month-old babies can retain information about colours and shapes around them for over twenty-four hours. Slightly older children show even more complex inherited abilities.

Psychologists also expend a great deal of effort on tracing the later development of speech, perceptual and intellectual abilities right through to old age. There is now a great deal of information on topics like memory, intelligence, creativity, personality and motivation. Generally speaking, the more psychologists find out about our individual abilities, the more impressed they are by the enormous potential of human beings. We

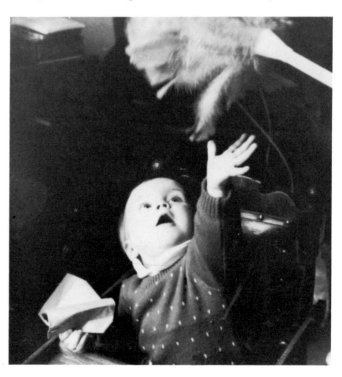

Unusual or novel stimuli attract a child's attention.

inherit and retain far more skills than most of us ever consciously realize and the capacity for enlargement and development of our abilities is much greater than most of us imagine.

Another major line of research and understanding in modern psychology is called social psychology. This reflects the belief that just as psychologists cannot predict the behaviour of people from knowing only about their physiology, they cannot predict that behaviour without taking into account all the various social influences on an individual. Human beings are highly sociable animals and most people spend most of their lives as members of one group or another. Psychologists have tried to discover how and under what conditions factors like early family experience, the membership of a particular group or the actions of leaders influence an individual's behaviour and attitudes. In Britain, psychologists like Michael Argyle at Oxford University have made comprehensive and detailed studies of many of the moment-to-moment interactions that take place between people in various social situations, and it is clear that these interactions have a vital and immediate influence on how the situation develops. It is also clear that there is great variability in people's ability to handle social interactions, and that these skills can have a powerful effect on their capacity to make and to maintain important intimate relationships.

Social relationships seem to be important to human beings, not only because we get from them our individual sense of identity, our purposes and our values, but because without these relationships we stand in great danger of becoming disturbed and distressed. Psychologists have now established that people who, for whatever reason, lack the support of relationships with others, are more likely to become ill or to suffer accidents, to have a poorer chance of recovery from illness, and on average even to die younger than those who feel secure in their social life. In Chapter 2, we look at the rapidly growing body of psychological knowledge which traces how individuals develop the social skills necessary to originate and maintain relationships. And we look at how people can be helped to cope when these skills are lacking.

Practical psychology

Increasingly, psychologists are exercising their experimental and statistical expertise to try and investigate everyday situations, and to see not only what they can learn about human behaviour, but what they can recommend to the rest of us, so that we can improve our effectiveness and happiness in real life. One major

Social relationships: the family.

growth area of this kind has been in the study of people at work, particularly in large organizations. Although the early industrial psychologists, the 'time and motion' men, were employed simply to discover how people could be made to work most efficiently, the major emphasis in modern occupational psychology is on trying to understand how all the factors in a job – the physical conditions, design of equipment, organization of authority, and the personality of the worker, etc. – combine to affect the health and happiness of individuals at work. Psychologists have now established that the wrong job, and the stress that goes with it, can make people seriously ill or even kill them. We discuss this and what psychologists think should be done about it, as well as the effects of unemployment, in Chapter 5.

In Chapter 3, we discuss the practical impact of psychologists' recent research into education and

The factory (above) and the dole queue (right). Psychologists are concerned to establish the factors affecting the health and happiness of both people who work and those who are unemployed.

teaching methods. A great deal of psychological research can now be combined to show that, particularly in secondary schools, much more could be done to release the potential for active, unthreatened learning and growth, which so many schoolchildren seem to lose during their early school years.

Another growth area in real-life research is the study of crime and punishment. Psychologists have established that there is a considerable gap between what we believe *should* happen when individuals are apprehended, interrogated, judged and punished and what actually *does* happen. There are many popular

myths about crime; for example, the belief that criminals are born not made, and that they consist of a narrow and easily recognizable class of cold-blooded vicious individuals who ought to be locked up for a long time in uncomfortable circumstances. In Chapter 6, we try to show that by the application of objective and dispassionate research techniques, psychologists have come to realize that the reality of crime in Britain is quite different from the impression we may get from the daily newspaper, and perhaps less disturbing.

By its very nature, systematic psychological research about human behaviour makes a quite different kind of assessment of everyday life from the normal human mixture of guess, gossip, coincidence and bias. A number of psychologists have recently turned their attention directly to the sources of bias in our cognitive processes and how these biases seem to predispose us to hasty judgements, ill-assessed probabilities and a dependence on stereotyped notions about each other. We examine some of this work in Chapter 4. As we now live in a society where we all have a capacity to do each other damage on a dramatic scale, this may well be the most important and urgent area in psychological research today. It is possible to bring together studies in personality, cognitive and social psychology and even physiological research to help build up a picture of the sources of the biases and prejudices so widespread in human thinking.

Finally, what many people want most from psychology is information and advice which can help

25

them to change themselves, especially if it can help them rid themselves of unwanted fears and bad habits. We have therefore devoted the final chapter of *All in the Mind* to research which throws light on how people can change. In a sense, change is the subject of the whole book, because we hope to convince non-psychologists that the more psychologists find out about the forces that constrain our behaviour, the easier it will become for everybody to make real free choices.

The information so far accumulated is paradoxical. On the one hand, the more research that psychologists carry out on the processes of perception, intellectual development and social ability, the more impressed they become by the widespread evidence of inherited mechanisms of control. These mechanisms reveal that far from being general-purpose learning and thinking machines, human beings have inherited very many precisely defined skills and abilities which clearly reflect the world we evolved to fit into. Even very tiny children are predisposed to interact in highly complex ways with their environment and the people around them, and this process continues as they grow up. So, the task facing parents and teachers is not so much to motivate or direct this growth, as to give children the room and opportunity to run through procedures they are naturally predisposed to follow.

On the other hand, it has also become clear that humans do learn certain notions of themselves and the appropriate behaviour they should use to respond to the world, and once acquired, these attitudes and habits tend to remain remarkably stable, despite changing circumstances and preferences. Unfortunately, for a variety of reasons, many of us develop strategies and habits for coping with the world around us that are ineffective or even counter-productive, and we would very much like to change them. Such ineffective behaviour ranges from stammering to heavy smoking, via dependence on a narrow and conservative approach to the world (see Chapter 4).

However, we very often find that changing our behaviour is beyond us, and that the very stability of our personality and habits has become a prison rather than a source of reassurance to us. Various groups of psychologists have tried to establish just how much we are inevitably constrained by our past and how they might develop ways to help us escape that past if we wish. As they do so, they are building up an exciting picture of the sources of human behaviour, from

conditioned habits to social pressures and reassurances, and from personal anxiety to an inherent drive to grow and achieve. They are also becoming more optimistic about our potential for growth and change at all stages of life. This book will give you a chance to decide whether you share their confidence and which of the techniques they have discovered may be useful in your life.

Smoking and drinking – two of the strategies most commonly used to help us cope with everyday life.

MAN THE SOCIAL ANIMAL 2

Man is the most social of all animals, so getting on with other people is a vital human skill. At the most basic level, we need to be able to attract a mate in order to reproduce ourselves, and children have a better chance of surviving and flourishing if they are cared for by two parents rather than one. Some behavioural scientists attach such importance to the process of *pair-bonding* that they believe all other human relationships are

Friends are important throughout life, but particularly so in adolescence and old age. In both these periods psychologists have linked psychiatric disorders with having few or no friends.

simply opportunities to polish up our social skills for the one relationship that really matters.

But psychologists have discovered that adaptive considerations and biological drives are only part of the story. Friends fulfil another vital function: they reassure us that we are likable and that our way of looking at the world is worthwhile. Without them, we should find it very difficult to cope with the fact that not everyone likes us or shares our opinions. At certain points of life, for example adolescence and old age, friends are a crucial prop to our self-esteem.

Research shows that friendship – like marriage – thrives on similarity, especially of attitude. 'Birds of a feather flock together' is a better principle to follow than 'the attraction of opposites' when selecting friends or a spouse. But the occasional row can be stimulating rather than destructive to either sort of relationship, and the process of living or working together inevitably raises practical problems and conflicts of interest which have to be argued out.

However, handling disagreements constructively can be a source of satisfaction and so can strengthen a relationship. Conflict is also to be expected when children become old enough to think independently, and feel compelled to challenge the attitudes and assumptions they previously accepted unquestioningly.

So a significant part of the knack of getting on with other people consists of being able to negotiate our way out of the occasional storm. But the rules of relationships also include knowing how to make ourselves attractive to someone we do not yet know well; judging how much to reveal about our feelings at different stages of a developing relationship; understanding that partners have loyalties to other relationships; and even realizing that different relationships have different natural life-spans, which means that some may need to be ended without causing too much offence.

We start life with many social advantages. Babies have a range of innate skills the only function of which is to make them irresistible to adults. And yet, by the time we reach maturity, four out of five people will have experienced crippling shyness or felt awkward with other people, and virtually no one is entirely satisfied with their social skills. In this chapter, we shall be trying to find out where we go wrong in the social game, and what can be done to put us back on the right track; in short, how we can learn to be liked.

Learning to understand the social world

As human beings we are deeply gratified by social life and very interested in making it work well for us. We try hard to maintain satisfying relationships. Yet everyone has experienced the grief, panic and self-accusation that follow from the disasters that are so common in relationships, particularly in the earlier years of life. And society is plagued by broken marriages, divorce, social isolation, unpopularity, and the blood-and-guts problems of people who cannot get on with one another.

What have psychologists done to explore these familiar human problems? What sort of work do they carry out to uncover the roots of such problems, to identify the reasons for success, and to help to correct the difficulties that some people experience? This chapter will look at the obvious (but, to some people, distasteful) possibility that successful relationships are difficult, skilled tasks that can be developed through practice. If this is right, then people with relationship problems could be trained to do the right things more often. Is friendship really like playing the piano? Is it sensible to assume that there are some very basic lessons to learn but that only a few people develop mastery? And is it true people can be trained to be better at relating?

One of the first explanations suggested for poor relationships in adulthood was disturbing childhood experiences. Everyone has now heard of the famous

Children's friendships. Games at school and in the adventure playground are important ways of learning about each other and the world outside.

maternal deprivation work by Dr John Bowlby: a deprived childhood, so the argument runs, leads to an impoverished adult who is incapable of good relations with other adults, and so may turn to drink or crime, or become a social misfit. But although it is now a surprisingly widespread belief that the relationship of an infant with its mother is a critical factor in its development as an adult, the idea, first proposed just forty or so years ago, is now being called into question by an increasing number of scientists. Is it a poor relationship between mother and infant that is responsible for the adult problems or are there other factors that matter? If so, what are they? Are other experiences in childhood able to reverse any of these tendencies, or is the early experience more important? And what exactly is it that the early experience influences, so that it adversely affects a person's relationships with other people?

A large body of recent research into personal relationships, coupled with increasingly sophisticated methods of investigation, now makes many psychologists suspect that the original proposition about deprived childhoods take too simple a view of the dynamics of relationships.

Among the reasons for challenging the idea are the problems scientists encountered when they seriously began gathering data on the subject. Certain evidence challenges the entire concept of maternal deprivation. One problem is that if you wait until you know whether or not a child has turned into a delinquent adult or is having relationship problems as an adult, the individual's memory of childhood is already ten or fifteen years old and rather unreliable. Such individuals may have a simple, biased view of their parents and childhood; they have probably forgotten a lot that happened; and their memory of events may not match those of other people. In particular, we are all likely to differ in our experiences of the *quality* of events and how they felt at the time; yet is is precisely the quality of childhood experience – poor quality in this case – that is supposed to have caused things to turn out badly for the adult. Some psychologists have also noted that people who are delinquent form a particular view of their childhood, bitterly blaming it for all their present troubles, whether or not it was actually responsible. Jack the Ripper may blame his crimes on his poor childhood because he is a bitter person, not because his childhood was truly deprived. And of course we would

never really be able to check on the truth of this.

Psychologists believe there are several other reasons why the idea of maternal deprivation is either wrong or simplistic. For one thing, it under-emphasizes a child's active role in shaping its relationships with other people and implies that children merely 'receive' what happens to them in a passive way (every parent would disagree!); for another it naively assumes that everything between the ages of about nine months and twenty-one years is irrelevant. Thirdly, researchers now have a better understanding of the ways in which children's relationships with each other, especially unpopularity at school, cause some of the adult problems that were previously blamed on maternal deprivation. Recent research has shown the critical effect of peer relations on children's development. Finally, as with many imprecise popular notions, advances in research techniques have helped psychologists to be more accurate in identifying the details that matter and to discover effective ways of putting things right.

Let us look briefly at some of this work. Working with monkeys, Harry Harlow found that those which had been deprived of maternal care or were isolated in

Doubt is now cast on the idea that maternal deprivation alone is responsible for such problems as alcoholism.

33

infancy were very disturbed, becoming withdrawn or aggressive and totally incapable of forming proper relationships – particularly sexual relationships – with other monkeys when they got older. However, he also found that if these deprived monkeys were put into groups of normal peers (monkeys of their own age) they began to relate in less bizarre ways; their adult relationships became more or less normal. These studies hold out the hope that the bad effects of poor parent-child relationships can be reversed or at least modified by later experience.

A young monkey which has grown up with a cloth-covered stand in place of its mother prefers it to the more 'realistic' dummy in its cage. Young monkeys separated from their mothers at birth often adopt this characteristic 'choo-choo' formation for mutual comfort.

In his work on children, Robert Hinde has found that although certain aspects of children's behaviour remain stable (for instance, their relationships with parents or teachers), other aspects are variable. Their confidence, for example, may depend on the person they are interacting with, not just on themselves (see interview, page 40). In short, we should not fall into the trap of assuming that a child has only one style of relating to people and that that is what is affected by early experience. Clearly the child learns something about itself and other people from its relationships with parents, but it also learns in other settings and the notions that it learns are different. These can affect its social relationships just as much as earlier experiences.

This work, and work like it by other psychologists, has helped to build up a more sophisticated picture of the nature of relationships, the kinds of influence that they have, and what aspects of the person's psychology they affect. Four basic aspects of relationships have been

shown to be affected by a child's early experiences with
its parents:

☐ The view it forms about itself as lovable or
unlovable – whether it sees itself as having a high
or low social value or attractiveness to other
people – is established then. This aspect most
probably *does* carry over to future relationships.

☐ Its style of interacting with other adults –
whether it is, say, submissive, trusting, hostile
or fearful – is affected. This aspect may also
carry over into later life, but is likely to act in
different ways, for instance by impairing
relationships with authority figures, but not
necessarily with peers.

☐ Its style of interaction with other children is
not yet formed, but the ground is laid.

☐ Its view of the nature of relationships is
shaped in general terms (nice/nasty;
reliable/unreliable; stable/unstable;
comfortable/uncomfortable). This will affect
general willingness to become involved in close
personal relationships. Suspicious people who
have learned not to trust other people obviously
find it hard to get into intimate relationships.

*Learning is an active
process which can be
stimulated by unusual or
difficult situations.*

Work of this kind takes us a lot further forward than
the original proposition of maternal deprivation. It
indicates important new areas of concern and shows the
variety of factors that need to be given attention for
relationships to work.

Children's friendships

Until recently the importance of children's friendships
was greatly underestimated. Researchers failed to
appreciate the significance of a child's need to learn
about relationships by playing an active role in a variety
of circumstances and with a wide range of people.

Adults who were unpopular as children suffer much
higher rates of alcoholism, delinquency, divorce,
difficulty with relationships, instability and psychiatric
disorder. Psychologists have shown that making friends
is a skill that can be taught.

Different methods are used to study children's friendships. Observing children at play shows what games they take part in, the kind of children they play with and the ease with which they get involved. Unpopular children are easy to identify. They behave like strangers; they hang around on the fringes of a group, watching but not joining in, scratching themselves anxiously, or they turn their back on playmates too much, giving out the message, 'Yes, I'm playing with you but I don't really know you. I'm not your friend.'

Interviewing children or asking them to write stories about friendship reveals what they think about friendship and their own friends. They are liable to find it hard to make friends if their ideas about friendship are sketchy, but they can be deliberately taught to develop clearer ideas. Three types of behaviour tend to lead to unpopularity: aggressiveness, social withdrawal and over-dependence.

☐ The aggressive child

Is hostile towards other children, has violent outbursts, is unfriendly, uncooperative and generally unpredictable.

☐ The socially withdrawn child

Acts as if all other children were strangers and does not try to get involved with them, but stands apart, doing nothing, perhaps sucking a thumb.

Both these children have failed to learn how to make friends with other children or have had such unpleasant experiences with other people that they cannot feel safe in relationships generally. They benefit from being taught how to approach others; how to do the right amount of smiling, looking and accepting; how to behave towards strangers by pretending to join a familiar group for the first time.

☐ The dependent child

Will not suggest games or take any initiative, is excessively shy, always follows other children and therefore seems boring and clinging. Playing with younger children, who naturally look up to them for leadership, can be helpful to such children because it gives them the experience of being accepted and in charge.

By helping children with such difficulties to make friends in this way, it is possible to prevent problems in the future which are both painful for the adult and costly to society.

Psychologist Steve Duck talked to a group of children in their playground.

Q Why do you think your friend likes you?
A I play tricks on her, and she likes my funny tricks, she always asks me to do them.

Q Why do you like Suzanne?
A She's nice. She's funny. She's always giggling... She's as small as a flea... And she's pretty.

Q Tell me why you like some of the people you like.
A I like Catherine because she lives near me and she often comes to play with us.

Q What do you think is the most important thing a friend should be like?
A They should be nice. They should be happy. And be kind. And play with each other. Help them if they fall over. Give you things. Sharing.

Most children get their first real taste of the social world in the playground, and for many it comes as a shock. Suddenly they find themselves surrounded by other children as eager for adult attention as they are, and there is no biological pull to make them attractive to the teacher. The teacher's attention and affection has to be worked for. So five-year-olds have to broaden their social horizons and make friendships with other children who are as socially inexperienced as they are.

Interview

PROFESSOR ROBERT HINDE FRS, Director of the Sub-Department of Animal Behaviour at Cambridge University, talks to John Nicholson about parents and children and the myth of the ideal relationship.

JOHN NICHOLSON Is there, or could there ever be, such a thing as a science of human relationships?

ROBERT HINDE We are at an exciting stage in psychology at the moment because a science of human interpersonal relationships is just developing. For a long time there has been a gap between the psychology of the individual and the psychology of groups which are studied by social psychologists and anthropologists, and now we're beginning to fill that gap. We need two things: to know how to describe relationships, and then we need principles about how relationships work.

JN Do relationships between mothers and babies set the pattern for all subsequent relationships for that child?

RH The mother-child relationship is, of course, a crucial determinant in the development of individual personality. This is not the same as saying that the mother-child relationship sets the pattern for future relationships, because individuals don't behave towards everyone as they behave towards their mothers. In fact, in our study of nursery-school-age children, comparing their behaviour in school with their behaviour with their mothers, we found surprisingly few similarities between the way in which the children behaved in nursery school and the way in which we observed them to behave with their mothers at home. But there were some meaningful patterns of correlations between the two which indicate that we can predict to some extent from the nature of the mother-child relationship how the child will behave in school.

JN Do you think it makes any sense to draw up or construct an ideal relationship between parents and children that we can prescribe to people?

RH No, I don't believe in ideal relationships simply because I believe that people are different and different people have different needs. There are, of course, certain general desirable qualities in the parent-child relationship. Mary Ainsworth and her colleagues have shown that sensitive mothering is very important for very young children, and that children who have sensitive mothering are more likely to have a sense of security and to be able to get on with their peers later on, will be better able to learn about their environment, and so on. But that doesn't mean to say that sensitive mothering is all. Control is also necessary. Control you can regard, if you like, as an aspect of sensitive mothering but, according to the circumstances, different degrees of control will be necessary.

JN Do you think we can learn anything about human relationships from studying animals, say, monkeys?

RH Human beings are so much more complicated than non-human species. So many issues arise with man that don't arise with a non-human species that one has got to study man himself. Having said that, there are certain lessons we can learn from the study of non-human primates. One is how very complicated their relationships are. And if their relationships can be so complicated without verbal communication, that puts a new perspective on our own relationships. Secondly, we can see how their different relationships are adapted in ways which make for the biological success of the individuals concerned. This is an important lesson to apply to human relationships because it ties together a lot of apparently independent facts that we now have about human relationships. One can understand, for instance, many things about the mother-child relationship if one views it as a coherent relationship that led to our success at 'evolutionary adaptiveness', as John Bowlby likes to call it; that is, in the environment to which the human species was originally adapted.

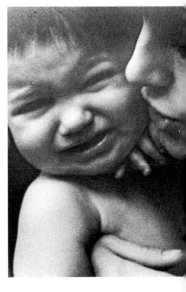

According to Robert Hinde, there is no such thing as the 'ideal' mother-child relationship, and parents should be aware of how differently each child responds.

Another issue is that the animal data make one a little chary of postulating an ideal human relationship or an ideal mother-child relationship. From a biological point of view, for instance, it pays an animal mother to wean her first-born infants relatively quickly so that she can have an opportunity to rear more. The more she wears herself out by looking after her first-born, the less able she is to look after her second-born. But with her last-born infant she can put her utmost into it, because she's not going to have any more. And not only is there an analogy with some aspects of human behaviour there, but it also demonstrates the ways in which relationships are shaped to serve the interest of the individuals concerned.

Another very important issue that comes up in part from the animal data is the way in which parents behave differently to sons and daughters. One reason is that, among animals, males have a very high variability in their reproductive success. Some males leave lots of offspring and other males leave none, whereas females have a much smaller variability; most females reproduce. More specifically, if you are a *healthy* mother, you'll have more grandchildren if you have mostly sons. But if you're not a very healthy mother, you'll have more grandchildren if you have mostly daughters. We know that this sort of issue in animals affects the care that the parent puts into rearing offspring of different sexes.

Now in man that issue probably arises, but there are other issues, too. Mothers, for instance, have different expectations about what is good for sons and what is good for daughters. In our work with nursery school children we've found that of those children we assessed as shy on the basis of an interview with the mother at home, the boys tended to have rather poor relationships with their mothers, but the girls tended to have rather good relationships with their mothers. In other words, the characteristic of shyness is acceptable to mothers in little girls, but not acceptable in little boys. Certain other characteristics like assertiveness and activity, moodiness and intensity are less acceptable in girls than in boys. And girls who have these characteristics have less good mother-child relationships than do boys with these characteristics.

But it is difficult to start making general rules about how parents should behave. There is the issue of sensitive responsiveness: some children respond in one way and some in another. For instance, if you have a child who wakes a lot at night or who cries a great deal, one child will respond to love, another will respond to control. There's another reason I think general rules are dangerous and that is that you can't be a good mother unless you're happy. The mother's happiness is an issue that has to be taken into consideration. It's very important that mothers should know that children are different from the time they're born, and that everything that happens is not their fault, but may be a part of the child itself.

Friendship through the ages

We have more friends at some times in our lives than others. Taken over a lifetime, the average for each person is 5.6 friends.

Age   **3 to 4**   Friendship is mostly about playing and is often based on the proximity of children's homes

5 to 6 Children say they are friends with someone because 'they help me', 'they do things for me' or 'they give me presents'; that is, friendship is based on egocentrism

8 to 10 Loyalty begins to be an important factor. Friends at this age help each other to develop; the basis is sharing, cooperating and doing things for each other

early adolescence Friendship is based on personality development, and many friendships are shortlived because changing personalities no longer support each other

late adolescence A friend enables one to develop, to be the kind of person one wants to be. There is a strong need for confidants; at about age seventeen the average number of friends is also seventeen – the highest ever. Friendship at this age involves trust, admiration, intimacy, loyalty and genuineness, but boys' friendships tend to be less intense than girls'. Having few friends is already associated with psychiatric disorders

early 20s This is the peak period for making life-long friendships, and it is also the most 'age exclusive' period of our lives (that is, most time is spent with people of the same age)

late 20s early 30s	The number of friends drops and the family takes over as the main source of social stimulation. The need for confidants weakens

40s	The number of friends rises again because we are now less worried about what other people think of us. Friendship is based on servicing and helping with the tasks of life. However, many men of this age say they have no close friends
post-retirement	Close friendships are very important: old people who have confidants are considerably less likely to become mentally disturbed than those who do not

Friends for life?

Michael Argyle

We know that everyone needs friends, but how do we, as adults, go about making and maintaining friendships? Friendship is all too often taken for granted and we give little thought to how it develops until things go wrong. In fact, however, it is rarely a random event. It follows predictable patterns and can be nurtured in specific ways, by following certain rules and applying the social skills outlined below.

The rules of friendship

Social psychologist Michael Argyle and his colleagues at Oxford University interviewed nearly a thousand people in four different countries about their attitudes to friendship. It transpired that, like other relationships, friendship is bound by rules, the breaking of which may place a strain on a friendship or even cause it to lapse.

People considered the most important rules of friendship to be those covering reciprocity (both emotional and material) and behaviour with third parties. Here is the list:

☐ **Try to repay debts, favours or compliments, no matter how small**

☐ **Share news of success with each other**

☐ **Show emotional support**

☐ **Volunteer help in time of need**

☐ **Strive to make each other happy while together**

☐ **Trust and confide in each other**

☐ **Do not criticize each other in public**

☐ **Stand up for the other person in their absence**

☐ **Be tolerant of each other's friends**

☐ **Do not be critical of other relationships**

☐ **Respect each other's privacy**

☐ **Do not nag**

Why do people become friends?

Let us take the case of two young women, Angela and Jean. They are likely to become friends if they meet frequently – for example, if they live near each other or work in the same place. Having similar attitudes, beliefs, interests and social backgrounds will also help. Their personalities should not be too alike (similarity of personality works in favour of marriage rather than friendship). Angela will like Jean more if Angela has a strong need for friendship; if Jean indicates that she likes Angela; or if Angela meets a friend of Jean's whom she likes. Meeting in pleasant surroundings and being in a good mood help to strengthen a growing friendship.

Life skills

As many as ten per cent of people are seriously handicapped in life by their inability to relate to others. Because, for some reason, they have failed to pick up the social skills on which most of us rely to get along with each other, they may be unable to make friends, or to make friends of the opposite sex, or to collaborate with people at work. The key time for developing skills is adolescence, because friends are viewed realistically then for the first time. But there is growing evidence that specific training in social skills can be helpful for people of all ages who have problems in relating.

Clinical psychologist Dougal Mackay has formulated the six basic rules of social interaction:

☐ **Impart feelings not cold facts**
In order to get the listener's attention, you should disclose emotions as well as facts. If you are asked, for example, what sort of work you do, give the other person an idea of the aspects of your work that you enjoy or dislike rather than just cataloguing your duties in a dry way.

☐ **It's not what you say but the way that you say it**
Most of us concentrate so hard at thinking of interesting things to say that we neglect our body language. Yet others judge us by our expressions, gestures and mannerisms in addition to our conversational skills. For instance, do not stand too close to anyone else, face the person head on, wave your arms around or speak in too loud a voice because this will

make the person feel uncomfortable. But standing like a statue, speaking in a monotone or avoiding a listener's gaze is a recipe for boredom. If you shift from one foot to another, fidget or look around too much, the other person will become anxious.

The appropriate behaviour largely depends on the situation and on how well you know the other person. Generally speaking, it is best to stand or sit at an angle about three feet away from the other person in a comfortable position, to move your head and body occasionally and to use gestures and facial expressions to emphasize the points you are making. In this way the listener will be relaxed and interested.

☐ **Know when to stop talking**

If you go on too long, the other person will 'switch off'. When the other person starts looking around briefly, shows signs of restlessness and stops nodding in agreement, you can be certain their interest is flagging.

☐ **Help the other person to start talking**

The more people tell you about themselves, the more they will like you. Ask them open-ended questions (such as 'How do you find living in London?') rather than closed ones (such as 'Where do you live?' or 'What do you do?') because closed questions give the impression of an interrogation and lead to uncomfortable silences.

Any interaction between people involves a whole range of non-verbal communication (body language) as well as conversational skills.

☐ **Help the other person to be self-disclosing**

They will be encouraged to keep talking and to disclose more if you nod in agreement, acknowledge what they are saying and show empathy by suggesting an emotion (e.g. 'You must be feeling quite upset').

☐ **Bring the conversation to a definite end**

Don't just let things fizzle out, because the other person will think you have exhausted your topics of conversation. And don't end abruptly by saying something like 'I've got to be going' because they will feel rejected. Instead, end by summarizing your exchange ('Well, it seems to me that you are in a difficult situation and I can

quite see why you want to change your job'),
reward the other person ('It was extremely
interesting talking to you') and give a reason for
breaking off ('I suppose we had better circulate',
'There's someone over there I want to catch
before he leaves').

How to recognize your ideal mate

Finding a mate is something that most people leave
largely to chance. However, the likelihood of success
can be enhanced if they know what they are looking for.
Dougal Mackay has devised a simple formula to help
you clarify the qualities you consider important in a
mate.

TEACH YOURSELF
YOU

Write down the names of six people you would not
marry under any circumstances. Then list the reasons
why you would not consider marrying each of these
people.

The idea is to establish your personal constructs.
Constructs are pairs of opposites (e.g. ugly/beautiful,
considerate/selfish) which people use to interpret the
world. Your constructs are your unique way of
evaluating people.

Now consider the qualities which are the *opposite* of
those on your list and you will have a fairly accurate
picture of the kind of person you are looking for in a
long-term relationship. Marital therapists find this a
much more reliable way of getting at the truth than the
simpler procedure of trying to list the positive qualities
you are looking for.

Marriage – what makes and breaks it

Marriage confers great benefits in terms of health and happiness (particularly for men, but for women too). But with one in three of this year's marriages likely to end in divorce, it is obviously important to understand the factors that bring people together and pull them apart. Stark finance, as well as compassion, dictates that we pay attention to marital breakdown: it is estimated that each of us pays about £3.50 per week to meet the cost of the social services bill for coping with the consequences of broken marriages. In human terms, poor relationships breed other poor relationships. Parents who do not get on are often too involved with their own problems to provide their children with the right grounding in social skills. This possibly explains why the children of divorced parents are more likely to have unstable marriages themselves.

Factors for success

Several studies have shown that those people whose marriages are most likely to succeed have a long engagement and get married comparatively late; have a reasonably good education and job but are not too ambitious; are flexible, emotionally open and not too dominant; are churchgoers, have no psychiatric disturbances and come from a stable home; and have a background and personality similar to that of their spouse.

Sources of satisfaction

Michael Argyle and Adrian Furnham found from their research that the three main factors contributing to success in marriage are: 'instrumental reward', which includes financial support and material help, advice and working together; emotional support; and shared interests. The marriage partner was far and away the most important source for all three kinds of satisfaction, rating higher than siblings, friends of the same sex, work associates or neighbours.

Ways of improving marriage

☐ **Follow the rules of friendship. These rules apply to all close relationships: respect privacy, keep confidences, stand up for the other person in their absence, be supportive.**

☐ **Show your appreciation in small but tangible ways (e.g. kisses, flowers, compliments).**

☐ **Do more sharing. Share feelings, activities and friends; discuss and work towards important goals; take adventurous holidays (shared stress can bring you closer).**

☐ **Face conflict and learn to negotiate. Be prepared to compromise. Use contracts to overcome differences.**

☐ **Communicate effectively. For more about using communication skills, see the next section, on marital therapy.**

Conflict: a shared activity

Argyle and Furnham found, not surprisingly perhaps, that being in bed together was the most characteristic activity shared by husband and wife. Next came watching TV and doing household chores. Arguing and intimate conversation were ninth on the list of twenty-six shared activities.

Conflict is common in marriage and can be compatible with a happy relationship. Half of all married couples admit they have difficulties in getting along with each other. But for a relationship to be close, partners must acknowledge and work through conflicts rather than avoid them. Happily married couples can settle arguments with less acrimony; they are able to discuss issues reasonably and constructively, and show a willingness to compromise. Conflict is normal, then, and need not damage a relationship; indeed, properly handled, it can be a source of strength. The most common sources of conflict in marriage are women's desire for more affection and more influence at home, and men's desire for more sex and a better-run home.

PSYCHOLOGY IN ACTION

Marital therapy

Most marriages break down not because the couple are fundamentally incompatible but because they fail to communicate properly with each other – which leads to frustration, friction and withdrawal – and because they entertain false beliefs and make false assumptions about each other.

Effective marital therapy must deal with both these aspects – the poor communication and the false beliefs – simultaneously. Dougal Mackay is a psychologist who uses this double approach to marriage difficulties. Known as the cognitive/social learning approach, it addresses the communication problems by teaching the couple social skills and the cognitive problem (attitudes and beliefs) by the process called cognitive restructuring, which involves changing the way situations are perceived. The television programme in which the couple Bill and Christine discussed their difficulties with Dougal Mackay focused on the first session, which dealt with communication skills.

Common communication errors are failing to state one's needs, stating one's needs too strongly, and failing to demonstrate that one has understood the other person's point of view. 'If he loved me, he would know how I feel' is the sort of statement someone might use to justify not stating their needs. 'I know she's not interested, so what's the point in talking about it?' is another example. It is not hard to see how this kind of reasoning can lead to difficulties.

On the other hand, if needs are stated too strongly, the results can be equally damaging. If one partner accuses, blames or criticizes the other, or over-generalizes – denigrating the other person's character – there will be one of two reactions. The other person will either respond in kind, which will inflame the situation and probably lead to a row, or will withdraw emotionally. Taking the case of Bill and Christine, both partners use blame and accusation freely. They also make communication more difficult, and breakdown more likely, by failing to show that they understand each other's point of view, making defensive comments that lead to further criticism and continuous interruptions which prevent the speaker from presenting their case clearly.

This small snatch of dialogue illustrates vividly how blame, criticism, defensive statements followed by further criticism, and frequent interruptions can lead to escalation of anger followed by a sense of despair.

Psychologist Dougal Mackay with Bill and Christine. The cognitive/ social learning approach to

marital therapy begins with the couple learning to listen to each other and to communicate properly.

Christine: *You came in with the smell of alcohol on your breath . . .*

Bill: *Yeah, I had a drink, you know . . .*

Christine: *Yeah, you come in, you sit down, put your feet on the table . . .*

Bill: *Well, what's the . . .*

Christine: *Then you switch on the television . . .*

Bill: *Well, listen, listen to you, listen . . .*

Christine: *I might as well be another cat.*

Bill: *Well, yeah, he's a bit more company as well.*

Christine: *That's great, isn't it, for all I do for you.*

Bill: *Well, you, well . . . Oh, what's the point in all this?*

This pattern of communication is common for Bill and Christine, who find it hard to listen to each other. In order to break the cycle of frustration in which they are caught, Mackay teaches them an important communication skill: saying how the other person's behaviour makes you feel, instead of making blame statements. Christine, from saying things like 'He just doesn't care. He's really selfish,' learns to say about Bill's coming home late, 'I feel concerned, I feel anxious and I feel lonely and I feel angry. And I think he doesn't care for me'.

Bill is then encouraged by the psychologist to restate what Christine has been saying so as to show he understands why she feels this way. After a few attempts he is able to do this without adding any criticism.

Only after both partners feel that their respective points of view have been understood and accepted can practical solutions be found to their problems. In later therapy sessions Dougal Mackay would engage with Bill and Christine in cognitive restructuring, encouraging them to examine deep-seated beliefs that one or other partner is rejecting or uncaring. In problem relationships such beliefs can persist despite a lack of evidence. For example, he would ask Christine, who claims Bill is cold and uncaring, to find alternative ways of explaining Bill's behaviour and to test the hypotheses she comes up with by trying out different ways of behaving.

In this way, two people who, as the therapist points out, want similar things from a relationship but whose ways of interacting leave them feeling emotionally isolated from each other can learn to relate more successfully.

MAN THE THINKING ANIMAL 3

We can only function successfully if we are able to make sense of the complex and demanding world we live in. To do so, we need to remember what has happened in the past, understand what is happening now, and be able to make sensible guesses about the likely consequences of our own and other people's actions in the future. We must also have the ability to learn that certain things are the case (i.e. acquire *facts*) and how to perform a huge variety of tasks (i.e. acquire *skills*).

The crucial mental processes are learning, remembering and making logical inferences. How well equipped are we for such intellectual activity? The short answer is – much better than we realize. Psychological research shows that we consistently underestimate our own mental powers and those of other people, especially those younger and older than ourselves.

Babies are much cleverer than we used to think. For example, they have an instinctive understanding that a sound usually means that there is something to look at and that objects are tangible. They are not wrapped up in their own little world. On the contrary, they try to make sense of the world around them, not just by passively watching it, but by actively carrying out experiments. These experiments include imitating adults' sounds and gestures, and even actions like throwing spoons on to the floor, which are sometimes misconstrued as provocative behaviour.

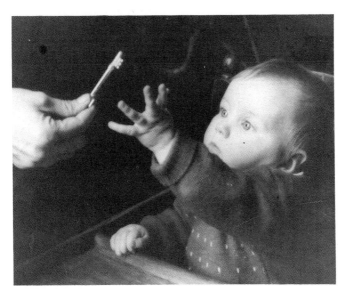

Psychologists have devised tests to ascertain the extent of babies' mental powers and have found them to be considerably greater than had previously been thought.

Young children, too, are often underrated as thinkers. The founding father of developmental psychology, Jean Piaget, insisted that before the age of seven or eight children cannot understand that other people have different points of view from their own, literally or metaphorically. He also maintained that children of this age cannot accept that objects can remain the same in one respect – for example, weight or volume – after being made to *look* different, say by being placed in a container of a different shape.

However, new research discussed in this chapter makes it clear that even young children are perfectly able

The test of conservation of volume, first suggested by the Swiss psychologist Jean Piaget, has been used extensively to test the capacity for logic in young children. The child is shown two identical containers containing identical amounts of liquid. The contents are then poured into two containers of different shapes.

Children usually say that the volume of water differs when in different containers. For years psychologists assumed that this meant children did not understand that the quantity of liquid remains the same, whatever the shape or size of the container. But now it has been suggested that perhaps the experiment is at fault, not the children being tested.

to practise the so-called *principle of invariance* and many other quite sophisticated logical skills, provided that intellectual problems are presented to them in terms which relate to *their* interests and concerns, and not those of the adult asking the questions.

The school system is supposed to build on children's natural curiosity and desire for understanding so as to provide them with the information and skills they will need to deal with the adult world. But many educationalists behave in ways which not only make it more difficult for children to learn but also create learning problems which may last for life. Detailed

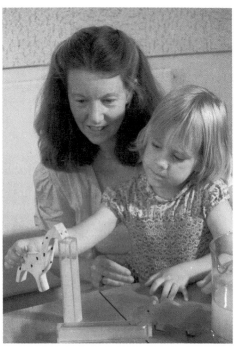

Psychologist Maggie Mills, of Bedford College, London University, is seen carrying out this experiment in a way which will capture the interest of young children. For instance, the girl in this sequence of pictures is at an age where fairness is important to her, especially when sharing things with friends. She is also very fond of animals.

When it is explained that the toy giraffe needs a tall glass to drink out of, she becomes interested in the experiment and shows that she understands perfectly well that appearances can be deceptive. In the right context she is already capable of quite sophisticated thinking.

analysis of what goes on in the classroom reveals that some of the difficulties adults have in acquiring new information and skills can be traced back to primary school days.

As adults we rarely make the most of our own minds. We regularly break the rules laid down in books like Alan Baddeley's *Your Memory: A User's Guide*, trying to learn the wrong material, in the wrong way, in the wrong frame of mind, at the wrong time of day. By discovering – and exploiting – the scientific principles on which learning and memory are based, and the intelligent use of such external memory aids as diaries and shopping lists, we can greatly increase our mental effectiveness – even in old age.

Boredom at school may have a lasting effect on a person's ability to learn and remember.

Popular fears about the effect of ageing on intelligence are based on a misconception. Research shows that although we do slow down mentally as we approach the end of our lives, becoming stupid or losing our grip on the world is *not* an inevitable consequence of the ageing process. On some measures, for example vocabulary, we may actually improve in the second half of life. Old dogs *can* be taught new tricks, provided that the teacher uses methods which exploit their experiences of life. In old age, intellectual functioning is closely related to physical health. But there is also truth in the old adage: if you don't want to lose it, use it.

Interview

DR GEORGE BUTTERWORTH, lecturer in developmental psychology at the University of Southampton, has been studying the way babies behave. Here he discusses his work with Martin Lucas.

MARTIN LUCAS   Could you tell me first what it is that you've been trying to find out.

GEORGE BUTTERWORTH   Well, in our experiments, we've been looking into the nature of the mind in very young babies – whether they perceive what's going on around them, and what they comprehend of the world and the people with whom they interact.

ML   And what kind of thing have you found out?

GB   We, and many other researchers throughout the world, have established over the last ten or fifteen years that even very young babies are extremely sophisticated in their perception and understanding of events in their environment. They interact in sophisticated ways with other people, and they can relate what they see to what they hear. They are able to communicate in very simple ways with adults, and with other children. All manner of abilities of this kind are being brought to light through very simple experiments.

ML   What kind of experiments have you done, and what kind of results have you got from them?

GB   We've looked at all sorts of abilities, for example the capacity to link what the baby hears with what it sees at birth. We've looked at newborn infants and have been able to show that when they hear a sound they'll look to see where it is coming from. We've also looked at the way that babies search for hidden objects, to establish how their memory develops. And, in a rather long series of experiments which I've been carrying out with the assistance of Lesley Grover, we've been looking at how babies and mothers communicate with one another from about six months to eighteen months, with respect to objects in the world around them. We set up a simple situation, and people might say that it's all terribly obvious. The mother and the baby sit in a small empty room, with just a few targets around, and the mother relaxes and interacts with the baby, just as she would at home. Every now and again she'll turn to look at one of the targets or to point at it and we establish whether or not the baby comprehends that the mother's pointing something out to it. We find that, as early as two months, babies can look where somebody else is looking and as they get older they gradually become able to comprehend the meaning of somebody else's gestures, such as pointing. Indeed they may point out the objects to the mothers themselves. So we see a reciprocal system, a system in which the mother and the baby interact, with respect to the world of objects. What's important about these experiments is that they demonstrate that even very young infants presuppose that they have something in common with other people, and this is obviously a necessary condition for the development of communication and language. What's surprising about it is that people for many years assumed that babies only slowly come to comprehend the world in the way that adults do; that is, containing things that are permanent and substantial and external to themselves. Yet here we have evidence that even very young babies will look where somebody else is looking, which presupposes that they behave as if the world contains the possibility, at least, of something that they may look at or interact with in common with adults.

Another implication of this kind of work is that if we think of the mother and the baby, or indeed any pair of human beings, as a system in interaction, we can see that even though the

In one of Dr Butterworth's experiments, a mother and baby are seated comfortably in a small room. The mother points out various 'targets' and even very small babies will look in the direction in which she is pointing.

adult is very much older, what they have in common is a kind of hard wiring, if you like, of the nervous system, whereby the processes of perception themselves presuppose that there is a world of objects out there to be perceived. We think it's this presupposition built into the nervous system that is at the root of those communicative abilities that one observes in mothers and babies. It's important, though, to remember that although that basic ability is built in, it develops very rapidly and one can observe all sorts of more sophisticated mechanisms become overlaid on the basic capacity to look where someone else is looking in the first eighteen months of life.

ML What kind of picture are you building up from these experiments?

GB Well, what's really most interesting about this very simple ability to look where someone else is looking is that it demonstrates, quite contrarily to what used to be thought, that babies are not totally self-centred, or egocentric, as the technical term would have it. They are able to take into account the fact that somebody else's point of view has changed, and alter their own viewpoint in order to see what it is the other person is looking at. This I think is the most basic and unexpected aspect of this ability.

ML Following that, as parents, is there anything that people ought to do that they don't, or should realize that they hadn't realized, when dealing with their children?

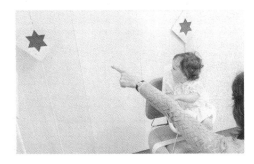 

GB I think the best thing that parents can do is simply to interact naturally with their babies, without worrying too much about it or being too self-conscious. Interaction is fundamental to the development of language and babies will develop normally, as long as they're treated as human beings capable of comprehending what goes on around them.

ML Would you say, in fact, that your overall impression of babies is that they're a great deal cleverer than we all thought?

GB Yes, I think that's absolutely right. Babies are a great deal more sophisticated, cleverer, if you like, than we have given them credit for. Perhaps what's happened is that psychologists have become a lot cleverer about babies.

Learning is active

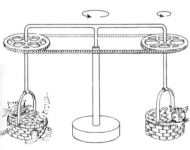

Held and Hein's kitten experiment. The kitten which is being carried learns much less than the one which is actively involved in carrying it around.

Learning is an active process. It is something done by people: it cannot be done to them. You can help another to learn, but you cannot make them. This is one of the most basic messages of the psychological study of learning, but its implications for education have still not been fully appreciated.

What do psychologists mean by saying 'Learning is an active process'? Perhaps the simplest way to explain is to say that learning is rather like eating. Food must be chewed, swallowed and digested; it must be broken down by the body before it can be incorporated into the body and put to use. Unless it is worked on, it cannot be used. Likewise, what we learn must be 'chewed over' before it can be integrated into our body of knowledge. Unless that integration occurs, we are not able to use what we are learning, and we are likely to lose track of it very quickly. The more efficiently and fully new knowledge is processed, the more 'nutrition', the more value, it provides.

How do we know that learning requires activity? First, because when people are not active they do not learn. Despite claims to the contrary, we now know that people cannot learn when they are asleep. So called 'sleep learning', for example from a tape-recorder by your pillow, only happens when you wake up. If the tape is turned off every time you wake, no learning occurs. Experiments with animals have shown that they too have to be actively involved in exploring their surroundings if they are to learn about them. In a classic experiment, Richard Held and Allan Hein showed that a kitten that is carried about learns much less than one which is allowed to explore for itself – just as a passenger in a car registers less about the route than the driver.

Secondly, when people are required to be actively involved in learning, rather than being just passive receivers, their learning improves. In one experiment by George Mandler, two groups of students were given a list of common words to study. One group were asked to *think* about the words, and the other group to *remember* them. When they were tested, the 'thinkers' recalled more words than those who were explicitly trying to remember them. In the same way, one of the best bits of advice for a student is to study with some questions in mind. When you are reading in order to answer a question, the information sticks much better. Simply trying to remember something is futile unless you are using your background knowledge to make sense of what you are learning.

What is the lesson of this research for schools? It is that children will learn better when they are actively listening – even if they are not trying to remember what they are being told. Teachers need to pay as much attention to helping the process of 'digestion' as they do to providing the right 'food for thought'. Teachers often see it as their job not simply to facilitate learning but to create it. We know, however, that the learner alone is responsible for learning taking place. The teacher should be there simply to assist.

Active involvement is the most efficient way to learn.

Anxiety and learning

Learning goes well when people feel challenged, and badly when they feel threatened. Whenever a learning task becomes threatening, both adults and children feel anxious, and anxiety interferes with the process of learning. A challenge stimulates people to learn; a threat inhibits them.

Psychological research has uncovered a variety of reasons to explain how anxiety is antagonistic to learning. First it provides a distraction. In order to learn well, you need to be attending closely to the task itself. But an anxious person is likely to be worrying about what will happen if they fail, to the detriment of their efforts to succeed. If your mind is full of thoughts such

as 'I'm sure I'm not going to do well in the test', or 'What will Mum say?', you will not do as well as you could.

Secondly, research shows that anxiety interferes with the learning processes directly. An anxious learner is more easily distracted – less able to concentrate on what is relevant and to shut out what is not. Every student is familiar with the difficulty of 'getting down to it', and the sudden attraction of tidying up, another cup of coffee, or the newspaper. For the apprehensive learner this problem is magnified. It also seems as if anxiety affects short-term memory, so that a learner can hold fewer things in his mind at a time. When the learning is difficult, and requires an understanding of how different facts or ideas fit together, this effect handicaps anxious students. Not only are they less confident, but their minds are also working less efficiently.

What might make a learner anxious? The most common kinds of threats are not physical but psychological: loss of self-esteem, being laughed at or feeling foolish, saying something stupid or being ignorant. For many people failure, or even the possibility of failure, is a major source of anxiety. Telling people that they are failing is actually the most common way of inducing anxiety in psychological experiments designed to investigate its effects.

Learning at school: the need for a safe environment

The implications of this research for education are very serious. The research tells us clearly that any place of learning needs to be designed to keep worry and threat down, and interest and involvement up; and it also tells us that one of the biggest causes of anxiety is the fear of failure. Yet schools, especially secondary schools, often seem to be the very places where the risks of failure are highest. Educational research shows that 'wrong answers' are very often greeted with a sarcastic or dismissive response by the teacher, and sometimes by the ridicule of other students.

When children's questions in class are not met with a judgemental response that implies they're right or wrong they ask more questions and more creative questions. But judgemental responses are perceived very much as a threat: learning is inhibited and the children become preoccupied not with learning but with defending their self-esteem.

The level of anxiety in schools may undermine the very function they are supposed to perform – that of helping young people to learn. Learning is intrinsically a risky business. It means giving up the security of what you already know and moving through a state of insecurity to a greater competence. It follows, then, that the most important part of a teacher's task is to keep background threat down to a minimum, so that children feel they are in a safe environment and have sufficient courage to be able to explore. This is particularly an issue in secondary schools, where there is not nearly enough done to create that safe environment.

Girls are most affected by this, particularly in subjects such as maths or science where, traditionally but with notable exceptions, they do not excel. Studies of classroom behaviour show that when a boy gives a wrong answer the teacher is likely to stay with him, suggesting new approaches to the problem until he gets it right. This encourages him to expect to give right answers if he tries hard enough and to see his initial failure as a challenge. Girls, on the other hand, are not encouraged to keep trying. If they give the wrong answer once, the teacher usually goes on to another pupil. Girls learn that failure in this area is beyond their control and not really their fault – this attitude is known as *learned helplessness* (it is, of course, not confined to girls) and often goes beyond the classroom. A girl can form the impression at an early age that her life is governed by forces beyond her control and some psychiatrists think that this is why clinical depression in adults is more common among women than men.

Both boys and girls can become 'infected' with the fear of failure at school and retain this fear in adult life, so that their willingness to take the risks that learning requires is permanently crippled and they are condemned to a life of playing it safe.

To say that teachers should pay attention to the way children are feeling, and to their prior knowledge and prior interests, is not simply a matter of liberal rhetoric, then: it is a matter of good, pragmatic psychology.

The teacher's role is now seen as one of supportive assistance.

With the right encouragement, girls can and do achieve as much as boys and overcome 'learned helplessness'.

Increase your memory power

Since the early 1870s, when the German philosopher Hermann Ebbinghaus (1850–1909) pioneered the study of memory by systematically teaching himself thousands of nonsense syllables, memory has been one of the most intensively studied areas of psychology. Ebbinghaus established that the amount learned is directly related to the time devoted to learning it, a principle known as the *total time hypothesis*. Broadly, this principle still holds true, but we now know from the mass of experiments conducted since his day that there are various ways of making learning and memory more efficient.

Rajan S. Mahaderan has a phenomenal memory. In July 1981, in Mangalore, India, he recited 31,8111 decimal places of pi at the rate of 156.7 digits per minute.

☐ Organize what you want to learn

The way you classify material affects how well you remember it. Because learning is an active process, the more you have to think about something, the easier it will be to remember (*see* Teach Yourself You, page 69). Mere repetition is not enough. Some sort of structure is needed to make sense of material. If you take notes by copying material word for word, you are missing an opportunity of learning the material thoroughly. By making notes in your own words and then turning them into essays, the same material passes through more stages and is more likely to be remembered.

Memory aids (mnemonic devices) work on the principle of organizing material by linking it to totally unrelated visual images. Others depend on rhymes or catch phrases.

The ability to organize increases with experience. One of the most striking examples of its role in memory is the ability of certain chess masters to play several games (against amateurs) simultaneously while blindfolded!

☐ Reproduce the mood and surroundings in which you learned something

Context dependency. Experiments with deep-sea divers revealed that things learned under water were recalled better under water.

According to the principle of *state dependency*, if you learn something in a particular mental state, you are best at recalling it in that state. This is why things learned after a couple of vodkas are also better recalled after a similar amount of alcohol than when sober. It is also why what you learn when you are sad you recall better when you're sad, and why, if you're depressed, you tend to be better at recalling depressing incidents from the past (which in turn make you more depressed). Clinical psychologists are now making use of this fact in treating depression.

Likewise, *context dependency* underlines the importance of physical surroundings: Dr Alan Baddeley found that deep-sea divers who had learned information underwater were better able to recall it underwater than on the beach!

Unfortunately, though, when it comes to remembering material for exams, revising in the room where you will take the exam is only of marginal benefit.

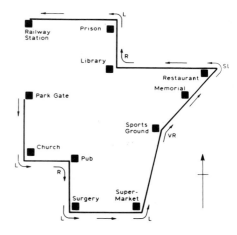

☐ Make the abstract concrete

All good teaching makes use of analogies, anecdotes and familiar examples to bring abstract thoughts to life, making them relevant and comprehensible. Use existing examples to anchor information in your mind, or better still create your own.

☐ Don't overdo it

When the new postcodes were introduced, Post Office workers had to learn to type. Experiments carried out for the Post Office showed that it took fewer hours of training to learn the keyboard if workers spent one hour a

State dependency. To test the effects of alcohol on memory, volunteers were divided into two groups and asked to memorize a simple route map. One group was given vodka and orange juice, the other straight orange juice. Both groups learned equally well. Tested on memory the following day, both groups again did equally well, provided that people were given the same amount to drink. In a different state they remembered less well.

Regular practice is the most efficient way to learn a musical instrument.

day at the task than if they spent two or, worse still, four. It took the group which spent four hours a day eighty hours to learn as much as the one-hour-a-day group achieved in fifty-five hours. The latter also continued to improve faster and after several months their standard was higher. This principle of *distributed practice* needs to be weighed, however, against practical considerations such as the need to achieve proficiency in a limited period of time.

☐ Choose the right time of day

As a general rule, if you need to remember something for no more than a few hours, you will remember it better if you learn it in the morning. Other things being equal, afternoon learning is usually more effective if it is long-term memory you are after. But it depends who you are and what it is you want to learn and subsequently remember. We tend to be better at more complex mental tasks, for example those involving logical reasoning, in the morning, whereas performance on more routine tasks like mental arithmetic may actually peak in the early evening. There are differences in personality, too. Some of us are definitely 'morning', and others just as definitely 'evening', people. As a rough guide, the more introverted you are, the more likely it is that you will be a 'morning' person. But it is safer to test your own efficiency at various times of the day, then try to plan your life so that, wherever possible, you find yourself carrying out the most demanding intellectual tasks at the time of day when you are usually at your best.

☐ Keep anxiety down to a reasonable level

A certain amount of arousal acts as a motivator, but too much is damaging to memory, especially if it distracts you by making you worry about your performance. The 'right' level of arousal depends on the individual and on the task in question. Extraverts, who naturally have a low level of nervous system arousal, may require more external arousal for optimum performance than introverts, who, because of a naturally high level of internal arousal, must restrict outside stimulation.

Questions of memory

The following test, adapted for the television series and discussed by Dr Michael Howe of Exeter University, is designed to show why we remember some things better than others.

Read through the following list of words and mentally answer the question next to each word.

Dr Michael Howe

speech	Is this a form of communication?
BRUSH	Is this written in small letters?
cheek	Does this rhyme with floor?
FENCE	Does this rhyme with tense?
FLAME	Is this something hot?
flour	Is this a kind of house?
honey	Is this written in small letters?
KNIFE	Does this rhyme with hunter?
glove	Is this written in small letters?
copper	Does this rhyme with mountain?
SHEEP	Is this an item of furniture?
MONK	Is this in capital letters?

Cover up this list and do not look at it again.

After an interval of about ten minutes, look through the list of twenty-four words on p. 75 and write down as many of the original twelve words as you can recognize.

You were asked to answer a question about each word in the original list. There were three different kinds of question – some about visual appearance (whether a word was in capital or small letters), some about sound (whether a word in the list rhymed with another word), and some about meaning (for instance, whether FLAME is something hot). Psychologists have shown that the likelihood of remembering something depends on the depth of processing involved in classifying it. The more thought that has to go into the classification, and the deeper the type of processing involved, the more likely it is that an item will be remembered.

Thus, paying attention simply to the visual appearance of an item is a superficial form of processing called *visual encoding*, which results in poor recall. Attending to sounds – *auditory encoding* – leads to somewhat better recall. But the richest and most long-lasting memory traces are produced by *semantic encoding*, when attention is paid to meaning, because this activity involves deeper mental processes.

For example, you will have almost certainly remembered at least one or two of these four words:

SPEECH	**FLAME**
FLOUR	**SHEEP**

because the questions you were asked about them related to their meaning (you do not necessarily have to be conscious of this process taking place).

Of the original twelve words it is less likely that you will have remembered the following:

CHEEK	**FENCE**
KNIFE	**COPPER**

because the questions you answered about them related to their sound.

And it is least likely that you will have remembered these words:

BRUSH	**HONEY**
GLOVE	**MONK**

because the questions about them concerned their appearance.

This experiment, then, demonstrates that when substantial amounts of information are stored in the memory, retrieval is influenced by how active we were in processing the information. So much information is stored that it is not surprising that we cannot always locate things quickly and easily when we want them. But without being able to retain and retrieve large amounts of information, we simply could not make sense of the world. The more active we are when we first receive the information, the more likely we are to be able to recall it.

Know your mind: memory and ageing

Memory does not exist simply to help us reminisce. It is an essential survival tool, without which we would be unable to learn anything and the simplest everyday task would be impossible. We need memory to tell us what to do next.

Our memories are remarkable not so much for the amount of information they contain as for the speed with which the information can be retrieved. It takes only a few hundred milliseconds to recognize one face out of thousands, or one object out of several hundreds of thousands. *Mastermind* contestants usually answer general knowledge questions in much less than one second. Our memories have to work at such speeds so that we can predict the immediate future on the basis of what has just happened. We need our memories to orient us in time and to execute complex everyday tasks.

Professor Patrick Rabbitt

It is a loss of these aspects of memory – fast access to information, fast recognition and fast orientation – that people complain about as they grow older. Professor Patrick Rabbitt at Manchester University takes these complaints seriously and is conducting a long-term study of how people's mental efficiency changes as they grow older. So far he has recruited a total of 2700 people, aged from fifty to eighty-six, and plans to involve another 4000. Each person fills in a questionnaire giving details of health, work, how mobile and active socially they are, how long-lived members of their family have been, and other background information. They are tested frequently for IQ, memory, motor skills and the speed of their reactions. They also complete a questionnaire to show whether or not they are depressed. Psychologists conducting the study obtain permission to have access to participants' medical records. In this way they hope to discover if changes in mental performance are paralleled by changes in health.

Using a variety of tasks, including chess problems,

71

computer games and simulated supermarket shopping, Professor Rabbitt and his team set out to answer these questions about memory: How justified are old people's complaints that their memories become less efficient with age? Can people judge correctly the extent to which their efficiency changes? Does age affect equally all kinds of memory (e.g. short- and long-term memory)?

How justified are old people's complaints that their memories become less efficient with age?

One school of thought holds that mental efficiency peaks in the 20s or 30s, then declines continuously, at first only slightly but increasingly fast in the 70s and 80s. Professor Rabbitt's preliminary findings, however, do not support this *continuous decline* theory. Instead, they support the theory that mental efficiency changes little, if at all, during life until a year or so before the end – the *plateau and drop* theory. Memory, he has found, does not necessarily grow worse with age. Knowing how old a person is does not tell you anything about their mental ability; but knowing their raw IQ score (that is, their IQ unadjusted for age) is very informative. Memory test scores and IQ seem to change together, not separately, which means that IQ and memory change at the same pace. Age affects the IQ test score of some, but by no means all, individuals. Professor Rabbitt has found, however, that healthy people manage to continue performing well, retaining high IQ scores and efficient memories well into their 70s and 80s. Evidence from Australia underlines this point: eighty volunteers aged between sixty-three and ninety were taught German using teaching methods specially devised to draw on their experiences in life. Within six months, half had reached the equivalent of O-level standard.

Can people judge correctly the extent to which their efficiency changes?

Professor Rabbitt set out to discover whether people worry unnecessarily about memory as they get older, or whether, perhaps, they are too optimistic because they are not aware how much they forget. He has found, by asking participants to rate their memory on a number of written tests, that people's estimates were not a good indication of their actual performance in their everyday lives or in memory tests.

The participants were also asked to estimate the change in memory efficiency they had noticed over the last thirty years. People who had noticed relatively little

Computer games (above) and written memory tests (right) are used as part of Manchester University's long-term study into how mental efficiency changes with age.

change did, in fact, perform better than those who thought that their memories had become much worse. Although people have no way of knowing their *absolute* levels of efficiency, this demonstrates that they can quite accurately assess changes in, for example, *relative* efficiency.

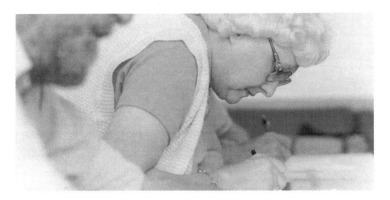

Does age affect equally all kinds of memory?

Old people often claim that their memory for very familiar or distant events remains unchanged, whereas they are prone to forget recent events. Rabbitt's findings indicate that in general different kinds of memory operate at similar levels of efficiency, so that if you are good at one kind of test, you are good at them all. IQ score is the best guide to overall performance.

☐ **Short-term or working memory**

This is needed to be able to remember and relate several pieces of information and to draw the correct inferences. It was noticeably impaired among the elderly and among those with hearing difficulties, whatever their age. The elderly seem particularly bad at remembering what has just happened or what they have just done, which makes it hard, in everyday situations, to work out what is going to happen next or what to do next. They performed worse than younger people at:

☐ Describing a familiar route from one location to another in a city they knew very well. If older people forget what they have just said, their directions become horribly garbled.

☐ Remembering television news broadcasts and weather forcasts. Even when they can repeat series of statements correctly word for word, they find it hard to combine the information from these statements so as to make correct inferences.

☐ Inspecting industrial equipment. They waste time because they forget what they have just inspected and cannot establish the relative importance of various tasks.

☐ Playing chess or solving chess problems. They forget that they have just analysed particular lines of play and therefore waste time re-analysing moves they have already considered. Because they are able to consider a smaller total of possibilities at one time than younger people, they appear less creative.

☐ **Long-term memory**

The elderly were less able than the young to remember all the buildings and shops on the street they had regularly walked along for years. However, people of seventy were just as efficient as those of fifty at remembering where particular items could be bought.

An important difference seems to be that, even when younger and older people have the same information in their memories, the former are more flexible in retrieving the information: they have more ways of retrieving it, and their memories are prompted by a greater number and variety of cues.

The general impression given by many studies of old age is that age inevitably takes its toll on personality and mental functioning. But the research of Professor Rabbitt and others indicates that whereas some people change a lot, other more fortunate people change very little and are able to maintain their memory and problem-solving abilities intact.

The experience of the elderly Australians who reached 'O'-level standard German within six months gives us all cause for hope. It is interesting not only because it shows that one is never too old to learn but also because of the reactions of the people involved: they were initially amazed by their rapid progress but soon revised their opinions of themselves. Their assessment of their abilities and of old age in general became much more optimistic.

Answers to memory test

Look at the list of words below and write down as many of the original twelve words as you can from the test on page 69.

WITCH	KNIFE	EARL
FENCE	WOOL	MONK
BRUTE	FLAME	SKULL
POND	HONEY	BODY
CHEEK	SPICE	SPEECH
NURSE	PAINTER	GLOVE
FLOUR	SHEEP	WATER
STAR	BRUSH	COPPER

ATTITUDES, BELIEFS AND PREJUDICES

4

We continually have to make judgements about other people and their intentions; we also have to make decisions and interpret what is happening around us. As a result, our formidable intellectual apparatus is constantly being tested, sometimes to breaking point – the phenomenon known as *cognitive overload*.

We have several techniques for reducing the burden. One of the most powerful is *selective attention*, the unconscious censoring mechanism which filters out most of the information impinging on our senses at any given moment. It best-guesses what we should be concentrating on, on the basis of which events have previously proved significant and which it is generally safe for us to ignore.

We also use *stereotypes*, which enable us to make snap categorizations of new people and situations before we know much about them, on the basis of certain key characteristics they share with others we have encountered in the past. Prejudgement – or *prejudice* as it is often called when the preliminary valuation is unfavourable – is a typical feature of human cognitive functioning. Certain kinds of prejudgements can even be useful, provided that the initial classification is treated as no more than a hypothesis which may have to be revised on the basis of later information. However, prejudgement becomes prejudice or *bigotry* when a stereotype is unjust or irrelevant, or when individual exceptions are not taken into account.

Prejudice and stereotypes form an important part of our *attitudes* towards the world and other people. But attitudes are surprisingly flexible. We are perfectly capable of changing the opinions we express to please the person we are with, and we seem to be untroubled by holding apparently inconsistent sets of values. Being racially prejudiced, for example, is not incompatible with having genuine personal friendships with individual members of a despised racial group. Even fundamental attitudes can be changed, though not easily. One of the most useful contributions of applied psychology has been the invention of role-playing and other psychological exercises designed to help us understand our own attitudes – an essential first step towards altering them – by showing us how the world

looks through the eyes of someone brought up in a
culture different from our own.

The roots of prejudice

When we talk of prejudice we are not talking of some
freakish, deviant trait to be found only in the
out-and-out bigot or political extremist. Human
decision-making is typically prejudiced in that it relies
on preconceptions, selection, bias and guesswork. Our
judgements are typically prejudgements. This is not to
say, though, that we constantly make mistakes. On the
contrary, we may often be very good at predicting what
will happen, at least in familiar situations. Because of
this we are able to react in generally adaptive and
appropriate ways to events in our environment. But we
also do sometimes make errors and categorize and react
to people and events in inappropriate and potentially
destructive ways. Our potential for 'prejudice' in the
common usage is thus part of our normal way of forming
judgements and decisions in an uncertain world.

The term 'prejudice' is used not only to describe
certain kinds of thought processes but also to express a
negative value-judgement about them. These different
senses of the word – the descriptive and the evaluative –
should be kept separate in one's mind. Nothing in what
follows should be taken as a moral justification for the
social manifestations of prejudice in the form of
discrimination on racial, religious, sexual or other
grounds. To say that a form of behaviour is morally
reprehensible, however, does not necessarily require the
assumption that the thought processes that underlie it
are different in kind from those underlying more
acceptable forms of behaviour.

The social context defines prejudice in the evaluative
sense. We cannot call attitudes or decisions 'prejudiced'
simply because they are selective. We cannot even do so
just because they are based selectively on certain
attributes, such as a person's race, religion or sex. The
appropriateness of judgements depends on their social
context, which makes the issue an ethical or political one
rather than a matter for psychology.

If, for instance, we are told that someone has been
refused a job on the basis of their religion, our first
reaction would probably be that this was an instance of
prejudice. Suppose, though, that we learned that the job
in question was to be head teacher of a Roman Catholic

school and the unlucky applicant was a Mormon. We might then take the view that it was appropriate in the context to take religion into account.

Ways of looking at prejudice

In the early 1950s there was a tendency to explain undesirable social behaviour from the point of view of individual personality traits and motives. The work of T.W.Adorno (author of the major study, *The Authoritarian Personality*, 1950) and others in the United States drew heavily on concepts from Freudian psychoanalysis to identify signs of authoritarianism, racism, anti-semitism and potential fascism in people's attitudes. Thus the main thrust of their argument was that prejudice and authoritarianism are evidence of a flawed personality, though even ordinary, upright American citizens were said to show evidence of potential fascism.

European research has tended to look at the mental processes as opposed to the personality factors at work in prejudice as a special case of a more general process of categorization. The influential work of the late Henri Tajfel views prejudice as a special case of a more general process of categorization. In dealing with people, this process means that we tend to categorize one another into groups and make inferences about each other on the basis of this grouping. For instance, on the strength of a bowler hat and pin-striped suit we might categorize someone as working in finance and infer, perhaps correctly, perhaps not, that he favours reducing income tax, cutting back the social services and increasing spending on defence.

Whereas American researchers were primarily concerned with categorization on the basis of race, Tajfel took the position that any feature, however trivial, could form the basis for grouping people. His *theory of social identity* holds that for categorization to lead to discrimination against outsiders, all that is necessary is for individuals to identify themselves as members of different groups, creating an 'us' and 'them' distinction, however trivial.

This *cognitive approach*, which sees prejudice as rooted in the way we process information, organize our thoughts and make decisions, also forms the basis of work currently being undertaken by Professor J. Richard Eiser of the University of Exeter.

Professor J. Richard Eiser

The cognitive approach

Our capacity to deal with the mass of information that bombards us from all sides is extremely limited. But we must be able to act in order to survive, and often have to make decisions on the basis of uncertainty. In order to be able to act in spite of uncertainty we rely on a number of cognitive strategies, identified by Professor Eiser as selective attention, categorization and commitment.

☐ Selective attention

Below: selective attention – making sense of the information that surrounds us and concentrating only on what is of immediate concern. Right: categorization – mentally sifting people into groups and 'types'. This process can simplify things for us, but it can be misleading and even dangerous. Here are some stereotypes and some surprises.

Instead of paying attention to all the information provided by our senses and from memory, we attend only to what we consider important or relevant to the decision we have to make. We concentrate on certain facts, personal features and aspects of events, and ignore others. For instance, when driving through town we may notice illuminated shop signs in a general sort of way but our reaction to them does not influence our driving (unless we are looking for a particular shop, of course). But we stop when we see a red traffic light because traffic lights are visual stimuli to which we have learned to pay selective attention.

☐ Categorization

Instead of spending time and thought on assessing things (objects, people, events or even simple physical stimuli) afresh each time, we group them into classes for convenience and speed. We view members of each class as more or less equivalent, disregarding differences within each class and emphasizing similarities. At the same time we see each class of things as distinct from other classes. A prime example of categorization is the use of stereotypes: thinking of people in terms of broad social categories, for instance, age, sex or occupation, can sometimes help one to make simpler overall descriptions of social events, but disguises individual differences.

☐ Commitment

We cannot know for sure that we are making accurate judgements, but if we allow this uncertainty to detain us we cannot act. We therefore suppress our uncertainty, acting on our inferences as if they were facts and in this way experience the world as more comfortable and controllable. There seems to be a mechanism whereby we stop thinking about something once we have made a decision. This is all very well in some areas (for instance, an indecisive driver can cause havoc), but in the context of thinking about people it may be risky, for first impressions can be misleading.

The tragic results of prejudice and fear.

Protecting our 'certainty'

We have said that the cognitive strategies we use help us to act in an uncertain world. By treating our inferences as knowledge we are able to increase our sense of control. But suppose we are confronted by someone who claims our 'knowledge' is wrong – that we have looked at the wrong 'facts' or looked at the facts in the wrong way. The experience can be acutely threatening. If others cannot see 'truths' that appear to us self-evident, our whole view of the world can be overturned. This is a threat that many people and many societies throughout history could not tolerate at any price. Within societies, heresy has been a capital offence. Between societies, differences in faith and ideology have been seen as justification for mass slaughter and enslavement.

Characteristic ploys, not always conscious, for protecting the certainty of our knowledge include:

☐ **Denigrating the oppositon**

Democratic societies stop short of murder to extinguish dissent. But if we can regard those who disagree with us as low in credibility, we can discount their disagreement as unimportant and are under no obligation to re-examine our own opinions. We can imply that our opponents are ill-informed, biased, irrational, even evil. Where the issue is important enough, those who disagree with us are viewed in group terms as 'the enemy'.

☐ **Stereotyping**

Akin to caricature in that they latch on to one aspect of the truth and exaggerate it at the expense of other features, stereotypes allow people to preserve the certainty of their own opinions. They are useful short-cuts in communication but, used negatively, they can provide an easy way of discounting opponents.

☐ **Denying contradictory evidence**

Denial is a primitive psychological mechanism designed to eliminate doubts. In an exaggerated form it can lead to disaster. For instance, Norman Dixon, author of *On the Psychology of Military Incompetence*, attributes famous military blunders in part to the officers' refusal to acknowledge the enemy's strength.

The current debate over nuclear power stations offers an interesting example of how these prejudiced ways of thinking operate. The pro-nuclear side seems genuinely puzzled that many environmentalists find nuclear power stations objectionable: either the anti-nuclear protestors are a bunch of unscientific romantics sporting beards and sandals, or they have been infiltrated by politically-motivated troublemakers, or both. Conversely, the anti-nuclear lobby seems to find the attitudes of its opponents just as incomprehensible, regarding them as materialistic, insensitive to human values, uncaring about the risks to people and to the environment.

Feelings over nuclear weapons run even higher. In Britain the Campaign for Nuclear Disarmament and other peace activists, such as the women fighting the deployment of cruise missiles at Greenham Common, are denigrated by the pro-nuclear side, including government ministers, as misguided idealists manipulated by Soviet interests. Proponents of nuclear weapons, meanwhile, are depicted as Machiavellian warmongers playing with people's lives for minimal strategic advantage.

Above: German Green Party politicians, apparent stereotypes within the West German Parliament. Left: women protestors at Greenham Common stereotyped by the popular press.

The counter-attack

Prejudice in general is very difficult to counteract because it is basic and largely instinctive. Counteracting it at a social – as opposed to an individual – level is a job for politicians, lawyers, social workers and other professionals. It is not possible to legislate against holding certain attitudes, but legislation can protect people from becoming victims of others' prejudice. This is the aim of the Sex Discrimination Act, for example, which makes it an offence to discriminate against men or women on the grounds of their sex.

In attempting to overcome prejudice at a personal level, perhaps the most important point to grasp and to convey to others is that certainty has very little objective basis. It is possible to hold attitudes with extreme certainty, to believe that one is correct and that one has absolute proof of the correctness of one's views; yet it is important to realize that other people can hold opposing attitudes with equal conviction and sincerity. Some individuals will never be able to understand the validity of their opponents' views. Some may not want to change their attitudes. But others will change their attitudes if they are presented with information in a way that does not make them feel wrong and therefore threatened.

Prejudgement becomes prejudice and bigotry in the Ku Klux Klan, which still flourishes despite strong opposition.

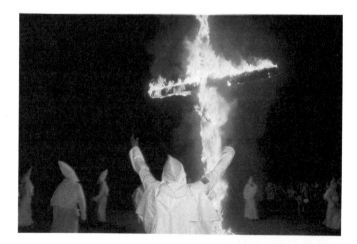

How conservative are you?

The following test, although too short to be scientifically valid, will give you some idea of how conservative (with a small c) you are. You may like to do it with other people and compare the results. Psychologists define conservatism as 'anxiety in the face of uncertainty', but it can express itself in attitudes towards the world and other people that seem anything but uncertain.

The following is a list of twelve social practices. Tick the ones you approve of.

1 Capital punishment

2 Racially mixed marriages

3 Using horoscopes

4 Modern art

5 Compulsory school uniforms

6 Working mothers

7 Censorship

8 Street demonstrations

9 Corporal punishment

10 Nudism

11 The current licensing laws

12 Drivers under twenty-one.

If most of the items ticked were preceded by odd numbers, you probably feel threatened by the uncertainties of modern life. But if most of your ticks were against even numbers, you are comparatively free of the strategy for concealing worry known as conservatism. People who score high on the odd numbers tend also to score high in tests of dogmatism, inflexibility and neuroticism, which casts doubt on the effectiveness of psychological conservatism as a means of coping with anxiety.

Interview

DR RAYMOND COCHRANE (above) and DR MICHAEL BILLIG (below) of the Department of Psychology at the University of Birmingham talk to John Nicholson about their work on the political views of young people and the light it sheds on logical inconsistency.

JOHN NICHOLSON How does your work differ from that of other psychologists?

RAYMOND COCHRANE Well, our work differs from traditional social psychology because we haven't relied exclusively on a formal questionnaire approach – which is how most people have looked at political attitudes – or done one-to-one interviews. We've used a group discussion method, whereby we start off a topic which we hope will gather some momentum in its own right, and the individuals will come out with the kinds of arguments, the kinds of beliefs, the kinds of attitudes that they would in normal conversation with their friends and colleagues and so on. And this has meant that the degree of flexibility in the attitudes they express is far greater than when you ask formal, consistent questions on a questionnaire. In that kind of approach you tend to get logical, consistent arguments; or if someone knows they're talking to a psychologist they're fairly guarded in what they say and they may be worried about how it is going to appear. But when they're speaking to their friends these defences slip, and we think we can find out a great deal about the underlying thought processes by, as it were, eavesdropping on private conversations within groups.

JN Can you give me some examples of what exactly you found using this method?

RC Well, we found in our examination of political beliefs that each person has a whole set of beliefs which are very often quite contradictory; that is, people can believe in one thing and believe in its opposite at the same time, and come out with 'A' or 'B' depending upon the nature of the argument they're engaged in. They don't feel any pressure to be formally consistent in their argument. So we found, for example, that the reason that people support a particular party has nothing to do, often, with the policies of that party. It has more to do with some emotional, symbolic attachment to the party. In fact they may hold beliefs quite different from the majority of the beliefs held by people who support that party, and that doesn't seem to worry them. That is, they don't feel any need to have a consistency between their individual beliefs on policy issues and their beliefs about which party is the best for the country. We've found people, for example, youngsters supporting the Labour party, who had very traditional Conservative beliefs about things. And on any measure that we took we would have predicted they would have been Conservative; in fact they said they were Labour. Equally, we've found a surprisingly large proportion of our sample of youngsters said they would support the SDP because they want a strong, authoritarian kind of government that won't bother with political arguments from the right and left, but will just get on and run the country and almost forget about democratic politics. They say things like, If politicians want to argue about politics, lock them up in a nice padded cell and let them get on with it and we'll get a strong leader to run the country meanwhile. Now, those kinds of views are probably anathema to the leaders of the SDP but nevertheless they are the kinds of views that have attracted a number of supporters.

JN   So, on the basis of all that, can you in a nutshell tell us what insight this has given you into the cognitive functioning of human beings?

RC   The insight that our work has given us into cognitive functioning is that it isn't the consistent, ordered, logical process that psychologists have often been tempted to believe it is. There isn't this pressure for internal consistency and logic. Cognitive functioning – and this applies not just to adolescents but to all of us, even psychologists – is a whole array of cognitions, beliefs, attitudes that we produce on demand, as it were. For example, when we're talking with one set of friends we'll say one thing, when we're talking with somebody else or talking about another issue we'll say something completely different. And that doesn't seem to worry us. Psychologists have always suggested that cognitive inconsistencies produce a motivation in the person to change one or other element until there's total consistency. We found no evidence for that at all. I'm sure if we'd used traditional interview techniques we would have found that, but when we observe what people say to each other in a relatively informal, unstructured situation, the theory of consistency seems to evaporate.

JN Michael Billig, what do you think it is about the National Front that attracts youngsters of the sort you talked to?

MICHAEL BILLIG One thing is that it's different, so youngsters who may be disillusioned with establishment parties and looking for something different, latch on to this symbol. The other thing that they know about the National Front is of course its racist politics. And there are deep feelings of racism within quite a number of the youngsters we talked to, the white youngsters. Many of them will say that they support the National Front although they know very little about it. It's a form of symbolic rather than actual politics. Often their racism is not totally consistent; they also have strands of tolerance intertwined with their strands of intolerance. Of course, if they were to join the National Front, these confusions would be resolved, at least

Extreme right-wing groups in Britain attract a large number of white youngsters, many of whom, Billig and Cochrane have found, have very vague ideas about what the groups stand for.

under pressure from the party; but many of the activists within the party think very differently from these youngsters who say that they support the National Front.

JN Is there anything about the National Front that attracts a certain sort of adult, then? Is there a typical National Front adult?

MB There's not so much a typical National Front adult. There have been people who have been attracted to the National Front or other fascist groups for a variety of reasons, obviously for racism, some for the aura of violence which attaches to the party. Some because they're confused and desperately want something new. And also there are the hard-core fanatical Nazi believers, who are very different from the casual recruits.

JN Finally, could I ask you what sort of insight into human nature, into the organization of human attitudes, has your research given you?

MB Well, if you examine the ideology of the National Front or speak to people who actually believe all the ideology, you realize the variety of ways of thinking. And the fact that people can always distort facts. It's not that we perceive the world in a simple way, but there are outside stimuli which hit our senses and produce an automatic response. If you wish to experience a world in a particular way, you can. You can push things to fit your preconceived beliefs.

Dr Mary Sissons of Sussex University has shown how prejudice can operate in daily life. In an experiment designed to examine helping behaviour, eight students – four men and four women – requested change for the telephone from white passers-by in Brighton. Of the students, two men and two women were Asian; the rest were white.

Patterns of giving help (defined as giving change or looking for it) were found to be affected by sex as well as by race. Interestingly, racial discrimination was found to operate only between people of the same sex. 'We didn't find a simple racism effect whereby English people, irrespective of their sex, gave less help to Asians irrespective of their sex. We found a complicated interaction,' said Dr Sissons. Thus, white English males gave most help to women – there was only a slight difference in the help given to white (100 per cent) and Asian women (92 per cent) – then to white men (83 per cent) and, a long way down the list, to Asian men (37 per cent). Similarly, white English women were more willing to help Asian men than Asian women. They gave most help to the white females (89 per cent), then to men of both races (81 per cent) and, finally, to Asian women (60 per cent).

In encounters with the opposite sex, the behaviour of the passers-by was

determined primarily by the sex of the student, not the race. Men, it has been suggested, enjoy the sexual innuendo in such encounters and were happy to help women, regardless of race. Women, however, were more likely to react negatively to the opposite sex, refusing help to men. In their dealings with other women, the question of race became important. When the sexual difference was missing, people were free to concentrate on other aspects of the situation and responded to the race of the person asking for help. 'In a same-sex encounter, where you don't have to worry about the social rules of how you treat someone as a member of the opposite sex asking you for help, then you're free to respond according to other dimensions. For example, race,' Dr Sissons notes, adding that the passers-by were probably not conscious of their motives.

Another interesting finding to emerge from this experiment was that the Asian students themselves did not realize that they were being discriminated against – they felt that when they were refused help, the passer-by genuinely did not have any change and knew without having to look. It was not until the figures for Asian students were compared with those for white students that the differences became clear.

The survival game

PSYCHOLOGY IN ACTION

All in the Mind visited Farnham Castle, home of the International Briefing Centre, where twenty-four employees of Shell Oil were taking part in a role-playing exercise called Survival as part of their training before being sent abroad. This is the sort of training that diplomats and staff of multinational companies go through in preparation for overseas assignments.

The Shell trainees are divided into two groups and told to imagine that they have just crashed in a small plane on the way to their destination. They find themselves in a totally uninhabited area, with no prospect of rescue. Their task is threefold. First they must plan for immediate survival, with the help of hand luggage, emergency supplies and equipment, a few tools and pieces of wreckage from the plane. Next, each group must draw up a plan that will enable them to go on living together indefinitely, establishing rules for their society and addressing such issues as distribution of work, the relationship of the sexes, education, treatment of the old, discipline, and acquisition of possessions. Lastly, each group must be prepared to explain and defend the rules of the culture they have created to the 'ambassadors' from the other group.

Although they do not know it, one group (the 'lush' group) has been briefed to plan for survival in lush, fertile country. The other (the 'arid' group) has been told its terrain is poor and arid.

'The probability is that the two groups will be in disagreement with each other,' predicts Peter Aylett, the course organizer, before the exercise takes place. 'Every society always thinks it's the best.'

The accuracy of his prediction soon becomes clear. Each group quickly develops its own *group identity*, which it defends in a frighteningly realistic way. On the basis of their ambassadors' reports the groups decide that there is virtually no scope for cooperation. All the elements of a clash of cultural values are in evidence. There are *misunderstandings* ('You've got us all wrong,' declare the arid group). Each side believes in its *cultural superiority* (lush group: 'We don't want *that* lot'; arid group: 'I don't thing that society is going to last'). And there is a fear of *cultural contamination* (arid group: 'If they influenced us with their happy-go-lucky existence, it might break down our society . . . ').

The people on arid terrain, who are in constant battle

Peter Aylett

with the elements, have evolved an organized, socialistic and highly moral culture in which possessions are pooled, leaders are democratically elected and all important decisions are taken communally. They have good medical facilities, they enjoy freedom of speech and movement and they prize their cultural heritage. There is no capital punishment or corporal punishment, but moral censure is strong. If a couple split up the fate of the children is decided by a committee, and the welfare of the group takes precedence over that of individual members.

The 'arid' group.

In the eyes of the 'lush' group, the 'arid' group is active, hard-working, time-oriented and efficient. But it is also smug, morally arrogant and, despite its egalitarian sentiments, aggressively competitive. 'We wouldn't like to live in their society,' is the verdict.

By contrast, the fertile terrain of the lush group has thrown up an easy-going society with minimal structure. Parents are free to teach their children whatever they choose, including their own language. Religious instruction is likewise a matter for parental choice. There is no formal marriage, and people are free to swap and choose partners. Members volunteer to perform tasks; the uncooperative are punished by not being fed.

The 'lush' group.

This *laissez-faire* lifestyle is condemned by the puritanical arid group as 'barbaric', 'behind the times', uncaring, chaotic and unstable. 'They seem disorganized, they have no set morals or rules to work from. They have no set structure,' exclaim the arid group in disbelief. How can a society that lives without the benefit of leaders, laws or calendars make any social progress? 'We feel we would like them to organize themselves in far more detail before we are prepared to trade or have any relations with them whatsoever,' is the arid group's uncompromising conclusion.

'Ambassadors' are exchanged.

If these harsh judgements are arrived at in a brief make-believe exercise between colleagues, it is not hard to see how cultural differences in the real world can lead to deadlock.

The value of the Survival exercise is that it forces participants to analyse deep-seated beliefs and attitudes they have not previously thought about and to realize the effect that cultural differences have on the way people interact. 'We should all be aware that we carry around this package of beliefs and values which gets in the way of arriving at decent solutions to problems,' says Peter Aylett. It is a lesson that Survival participants, who have 'put themselves on the line', are not likely to forget.

The final session.

WORK: DO WE NEED IT?

Research by occupational psychologists helps us to understand the paradox that we can be harmed – mentally and physically – both by working and by not working. Unemployment and overwork are both associated with stress (anything that requires us to change or adapt ourselves is defined as a stressor), but different people respond very differently to being put under pressure. Some thrive on it, others crack. Psychological tests can be used to prevent round pegs being selected for square holes – perhaps the major cause of stress at work. Psychologists can also advise employers on how to minimize organizational stress.

Involuntary unemployment is one of the most feared conditions of our age. Psychologists have made considerable progress towards understanding why it is so aversive, and what sort of people suffer most when forced to give up their jobs. However, a certain small group of individuals seem unusually well-equipped to deal with life without work, and it may be that closer examination of their behaviour can help us plan for a future in which there may be no formal paid employment available for a significant proportion of the working-age population.

As far as the present is concerned, there is evidence that a management style based on sound psychological ⸱⸱ciples, with a declared interest in meeting human ⸱⸱ ⸱s as well as profit forecasts, can produce the goods – as well as a healthier and more contented work force.

Support in the workplace

Some people thrive on stress, deriving enjoyment and satisfaction from challenge and pressure. But for many of us, stress at work can culminate in ill health and heart disease. Psychologists are beginning to understand what makes some jobs more stressful than others and what can be done in the workplace to minimize the damage.

We all know how much we rely on the support of friends and how important they are in our daily lives. Research shows that friendships are also important at work, being largely responsible for feelings of job satisfaction and for providing informal support in the workplace where no formal support is offered by the employers. In their book *Understanding Executive Stress*,

Cary Cooper and Judy Marshall put forward substantial evidence of how social groups may provide the kind of support that can reduce stress and the risk of heart disease.

Organized support

Work organizations vary in the social support systems they provide for their employees. The term 'social support' as used here encompasses *cognitive support* (advice and exchange of information), *emotional support*, and *behavioural* (i.e. practical) *support*.

Roy Payne of Sheffield University has suggested a framework for understanding the subject. He contrasts the formal organization (one dominated by rules, regulations, hierarchies and specialists), in which the employee is largely on the receiving end of support, with the less structured informal organization, in which support is a two-way transaction and employees both give and receive it. In the former, the emphasis is on provision of facilities and inducements; in the latter, it is on exchange and interaction. Thus, in the formal organization, advice and emotional support are dispensed by experts – doctors, counsellors, consultants, occupational health nurses and welfare officers. In the informal organization, on the other hand, problems are solved by pooling resources and information; if experts play a part, they are likely to be known personally to the group members. Emotional support is marshalled spontaneously by the group, and the recipient is more likely to feel that it is genuine. On the practical level, formal organizations are likely to demonstrate their support for employees under stress by relieving them of responsibility, taking them off the job, helping them to change jobs or arranging for early retirement; alternatively, they may find someone else to solve the problem. Practical support in the informal organization more probably takes the form of helping employees to do the job, or of doing it for them while they recover. Responsibility is *shared* not *removed*.

Work organizations *can* provide cognitive, emotional and behavioural support for their workers, but do they? Most provide only nominal cognitive support in the form of advice on topics such as safety. A few, like Pepsico Inc., provide complete fitness and health facilities for their employees. Emotional support is rarely given attention by managements and is more likely to be provided by the workers themselves.

Worker participation

As early as in the 1940s Coch and French explored the impact of greater involvement and participation at work in a study of three kinds of participation in a sewing factory. They found the greater the participation the higher the productivity, and the greater the job satisfaction, the lower the turnover of staff and the better the relationships between boss and subordinates. These findings have been supported by many later studies.

Volvo is one of the most talked-about worker-participation projects in the world. At their Kalmar works, 10 per cent was added to building costs at the planning stage so that the assembly plant could accommodate principles of worker participation.

In the metal-pressing section, for example, workers wear uniforms coloured according to their job. Jobs are rotated, and the quota is agreed by the planning department and the union. No overtime is paid: employees work until the quota is met but if they finish early they can take a swim or sauna at the plant.

In the body-finishing section, there are several lines of work, each with its own characteristics. In one line the workers follow the cars on the conveyor and do each job as the car progresses past various tool stations. On other lines, the workers stand in place and the car passes by. Workers use a variety of job-rotating schemes to assemble the car. Some lines have workers in uniforms and others have workers in their own clothes; workers make their own decisions about this.

This small Volvo team works in a clean and spacious environment quite unlike the traditional cog-in-a-wheel production line.

In the truck-assembly section, the work is done in small teams of eight or ten, with all the parts and tools available to assemble a complete unit. Workers elect their own supervisors, who are paid a marginally higher wage but can be replaced by a vote of confidence at any time. Replacement workers are brought in by consent. The team trains the new workers and brings them up to standard.

Volvo is an assembly operation on twenty-one sites; 650 sub-contractors make the components. The corporate level has special divisions to lend support and finance, if necessary, to the subcontractors to help them maintain their profits and standards. There is no policy of amalgamating the contractors into a vertical manufacturing system as has been done in most other motor industries.

Emotional support

There is a clear-cut failure on the part of most organizations to give emotional support to their workers. Very few private or public sector institutions provide adequate social support systems. When work does provide social support, it is usually through an *informal* network. For a long time it was felt that it was beyond the scope of organizations to provide counsellors or psychiatric social workers or other sources of human support for employees, particularly if their problems stemmed from the home environment, even when these affected the person at work. But it is increasingly difficult to draw a clear line between sources of stress. In addition, two other factors are forcing organizations to take an interest in providing social support systems at work: one is the increasing amount of litigation, particularly in America, against companies for stress illnesses alleged to have originated in the workplace; the other is the increasing incidence of stress-like epidemics in factories and offices which have led to widespread absenteeism.

The first phenomenon is known as *cumulative trauma*, which is a type of workers' compensation claim in which an employee contends that a major illness or disability is the cumulative result of minor job stresses and strains stretching back over a period of years. Any working person, from the shopfloor to the boardroom, if forced to give up work as a result of any type of illness (for instance, coronary heart disease, mental breakdown, nervous debility) can claim that this was caused by the stress of work over a period of years. Since it is relatively

Employee Advisory Resource, a scheme started by Control Data in the USA to provide care for its own employees, is now in demand as a service to other companies.

easy to show that just about any job has a certain element of stress in it and since the law in various American states allows a very liberal interpretation of stress-induced illness, the courts and appeal boards are accepting many of these claims. More importantly, the organizations involved are, in many cases, unable to provide evidence that they are trying to minimize the stresses and strains of the work environment. Years of neglect of the wellbeing of staff have finally caught up with those responsible, who are being forced to pay more attention to and provide more facilities for stress prevention.

The second phenomenon is what the National Institute for Occupational Safety and Health in the United States terms *mass psychogenic illness*. This is a situation in which a number of workers in a particular plant or factory develop a mysterious disease, with no clearly identified microorganism at its source. Specific symptoms vary from one industrial situation to another but they usually consist of subjective somatic complaints, such as headaches, nausea, lethargy and chills. In all cases extensive biochemical and environmental tests (to check for harmful chemicals in the air) have been carried out and nothing found. However, all these work environments have been found to be highly stressful and to lack social support systems.

As a result of pressures like these, there are an increasing number of stress-prevention programmes aiming to provide emotional support. For example, one large copper corporation has focused on the psychological health of all its employees by providing extensive counselling facilities for all work and personal problems, even arranging Alcoholics Anonymous groups for employees and their families. A company in Massachusetts which introduced a voluntary programme found that relaxation breaks improved employees' health, standard of work and wellbeing as well as significantly lowering their blood pressure in a matter of weeks.

In Britain, at least one large chemical company has set up an employee counselling service using a full-time counsellor with a background in psychiatric social work. It aims to provide a confidential counselling service to all employees and their families, to work with outside helping professions for the welfare of the employee, and to provide other activities that enhance the quality of working life. After four years, the counsellor has been consulted by nearly 10 per cent of the employees each year. About half of these seek advice on education, family matters, work-related housing problems, divorce, separation, children, aged parents and consumer affairs. The other half consult the counsellor regularly for help with longer-term personal and relationship problems.

Work-related stress

In 1983 the United Kingdom had the unenviable distinction of surpassing Finland to become the country with the highest rate of death from heart disease in the world. Whereas in the United States the number of people who died from heart disease dropped by more than 20 per cent between 1970 and 1977, in the UK the number increased by more than 10 per cent over the same period.

Heart disease is the most dramatic manifestation of stress, but there are less serious ones, such as ulcers, back pain and headaches, which make many people's lives a misery and cost industry millions of working days each year. Psychologists and other professionals are beginning to discern the patterns of stress at work – who gets it, the conditions likely to foster it and the steps that can be taken to minimize it.

Your life in their hands – the stress of great responsibility.

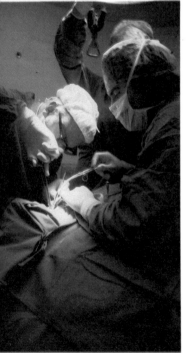

Stressful occupations

Certain jobs are obviously more stressful than others: air traffic controllers, for instance, suffer more stress-related diseases such as ulcers and high blood pressure, and at an earlier age, than the rest of the population; policemen in the US are more than twice as likely as the average male city-dweller to commit suicide. Long periods of inactivity alternating with short bursts of intense activity demanding wholehearted concentration make a pilot's life particularly stressful. The pressure of the pilot's job comes from cognitive strain – the need to process a lot of information from different sources simultaneously (*see* 'The danger of cognitive overload' later in this chapter) – combined with responsibility for the lives of others and for equipment worth millions of pounds.

Also at risk of work-related stress is anyone who has to make life-and-death decisions (surgeons, firemen); who is exposed to danger (miners, trawlermen) or high levels of noise (pneumatic drill operators, blast-furnace workers); or who has irregular sleep patterns (shift-workers, doctors and nurses). Even mothers at home with young children suffer their share of stress – they have to be constantly vigilant, have little or no time for breaks, and must endure the noise of children as well as of domestic appliances.

From pineapple packing to air traffic control – stress at work can arise from many different causes.

The stress-prone personality

Some people leap out of bed, bolt down breakfast while they read their post (if they find time to eat breakfast at all), and shave in the car on the way to work while listening to the news on the radio and mentally drawing up a list of tasks to accomplish. Their whole day is one long rush from job to job, or from meeting to meeting, fretting about how much has to be done in the short time available, fuming over delays, tapping their feet in queues, flitting from one idea to the next, cutting people off in mid-sentence or finishing their sentences for them. Life is one long simmer, just below boiling point, until a heart attack forces them to stop.

This aggressive, hard-driving, time-conscious, irritable individual, whose response to stress makes him a likely candidate for a heart attack, was first classified by the American cardiologists Ray H. Rosenman and Meyer Friedman, who dubbed him the Type A personality. Their book *Type A Behavior and Your Heart* contrasts his behaviour (or hers – women's rise up the management ladder is turning them more and more into Type As) with that of the Type B individual, whose approach to life and work is more patient, relaxed and contemplative, and altogether less aggressive.

Temperament and culture largely dictate whether you are a Type A or a Type B person. Some people are naturally more competitive than others, and different cultures have different values. The United States is predominantly a Type A culture, Scandinavia and Japan Type B. But there is nothing fixed about these categories. Women, traditionally Type B personalities, are becoming increasingly hard-driving – and prone to heart disease – as they compete with Type A men in the business world. Conversely, the worst excesses of Type A behaviour can be toned down by deliberate stress-reduction programmes, involving relaxation, meditation, biofeedback or autogenics, as well as by changes in lifestyle and attitude.

The Instant Stress Detector quiz on page 109 should give you an idea of whether or not you are likely to become a victim of stress.

Stressful styles of management

One of the reasons that deaths from heart attacks are increasing in Britain, in the opinion of Cary Cooper, Professor of Organizational Psychology at Manchester University, is that the British have begun to emulate the American example of deliberately trying to create Type

A environments – environments that are competitive and time-conscious, where people are expected to work long hours as a matter of course. This management policy is based on the assumption that Type A behaviour helps productivity. In fact, the reverse is true. Japan, whose accent on tradition, courtesy and social support makes it a classic Type B culture, is not only one of the most productive countries in the world but also has the lowest incidence of coronary heart disease.

Many people in the West, Professor Cooper points out, ridicule the Japanese organization man, but it is the very structures of Japanese corporate life – shared decision-making, group affiliations, corporate identity, group counselling and so on – that help prevent stress-related disease. This health-promoting quality of Japanese life has been confirmed in a large-scale study conducted at the University of California showing that Japanese living in the United States suffered twice as much coronary heart disease as Japanese in Japan, although other risk factors – like cholesterol levels, smoking and blood pressure – were similar in the two groups. The researchers attribute these differences to the extent to which Japanese Americans have abandoned their traditional way of life, losing their social supports at home and work as they form mobile, nuclear families and adopt the American pace of living.

A shop for employees at the Toyota car factory in Japan.

The quality of the relationship between you and your boss is fundamental to health and job satisfaction. The worse the relationship, the more likely you are to suffer from stress. In Britain, where the style of management tends to be autocratic, employees are likely to complain that they have no control over their work, that their boss doesn't value them sufficiently, or that he is constantly looking over their shoulder. Still, these complaints are heard less often in those companies (*see* Psychology in Action, page 115) which have followed the example of the Scandinavians and Japanese by setting up autonomous work groups and encouraging worker participation.

'The most important thing is for people to feel that they have control over their work,' says Professor Cooper. 'They need to feel that they can be rewarded. We too frequently manage people by punishment rather than by reward and praise.'

Women in management

The participative approach to management comes more naturally to women. Studies by the Manpower Research Commission and research organizations throughout the world are showing that women's style of management is often less controlling, more caring and more supportive than that of men. As more and more women enter the management field, Professor Cooper predicts that the atmosphere in business may become less stressful. In the meantime, however, women are increasingly afflicted by stress-related conditions – anxiety, depression, migraines, poor sleep – from the strain of managing both career and home, particularly in the United Kingdom, where working wives receive little support in the home.

Women are not alone in paying a high price for challenging traditional roles. From Framingham, the Massachusetts community that is the subject of a long-term study of heart disease, comes news that being married to a successful woman greatly increases the coronary risk for a man in his middle or later years. Studying couples over a ten-year period, the Framingham researchers have shown that men aged 45 to 64 are three to five times more likely to develop coronary heart disease if their wives have high-flying careers than if they are clerical or manual workers. Professor Cooper lays the onus on men's psychological rigidity in clinging to outworn stereotypes of male and female behaviour. 'What has to be driven home,' he

A Congresswoman in the USA.

notes, 'is that there is no need to change the women.
Men have to be trained into adopting a different
perspective for the better health of everybody.'

Women's style of management is not only more
supportive – it may even be more productive. Professor
Cooper believes that most women are less ambitious
than men but better managers. His own research shows
that male employees concur with him: most consider
their female bosses to be better at managing people.

How to reduce stress at work

As we have shown, certain management styles are
more effective in minimizing stress than others. But
whatever the company policy, the behaviour of
supervisors is instrumental in setting the tone for
relations in the workplace. Social psychologist Michael
Argyle has found in his research on relationships that
health and job satisfaction are enhanced when
supervisors are supportive and friendly, care about
employees' welfare, consult them about decisions and
explain and persuade rather than merely give orders.
Here are his guidelines for supervisors:

☐ **Plan and assign work efficiently.**

☐ **Keep subordinates informed about
decisions affecting them.**

☐ **Respect privacy.**

☐ **Keep confidences.**

☐ **Consult subordinates about matters that
affect them.**

☐ **Advise and encourage subordinates.**

☐ **Fight for subordinates' interests.**

☐ **Be considerate about personal problems.**

On an individual level, there are steps that you can take to avoid falling into the trap of damaging Type A behaviour. For example:

☐ **Set goals and priorities. There isn't time to do everything. Do the essentials, delegate what you can and forgo the rest.**

☐ **Do only one thing at a time.**

☐ **Don't expect perfection in yourself or others. It will just make you frustrated and hostile.**

☐ **Take periodic breaks, even when working to a deadline.**

☐ **Spend some time alone each day doing nothing, even if for only a few minutes.**

☐ **Relieve stress through exercise, relaxation, laughter, pleasurable activities.**

☐ **Do not feel you always have to be right.**

☐ **Give more thought to the needs of others.**

The danger of cognitive overload

Dr Donald Broadbent

Most of the stress we have been talking about is emotional stress. But, strictly speaking, any situation that forces us to adapt or change ourselves is stressful.

One damaging form of externally induced stress is the *cognitive overload* to which airline pilots and air traffic controllers, among others, are particularly vulnerable. Anyone who must process a lot of information from different sources simultaneously in order to make critical decisions can fall victim to cognitive overload, in which the requirements of one task interfere with those of other, competing, tasks. This interference is particularly likely between two tasks if both make use of the same sense-organ or the same hand.

Dr Donald Broadbent, former Director of the Medical Research Council Applied Psychology Unit at Cambridge University, has spent many years studying how quickly people can process information and how

different tasks, such as listening to speech, reading and operating controls, interact with one other. His starting point is the practical problems people encounter in their jobs. By simulating their work conditions in his laboratory he can examine the way people process information and make decisions. He may, for instance, flash an image or digits quickly before their eyes at the same time as playing a tape-recorded message or asking them to remember lists of items. He studies how long it takes a person to press a button when there are several possibilities and the effect that competing demands and different ways of presenting information have on performance and memory. His aim is to devise work environments that minimize interference between tasks and facilitate integration, so that employees make fewer mistakes, and are more satisfied and productive.

The element of the unexpected contributes to cognitive overload. 'The less surprising the things you have to do and the things that happen, the more you can deal with them at the same time as you can do other things,' he says. The problem for pilots, whose work Dr Broadbent has been studying, is 'largely a matter of reacting to the unexpected'. The pilot must analyse and take decisions on the basis of both what he hears through his headphones and what he sees on his instrument panel, and the unexpected is almost routine.

'Reaching the right decision about two sources of information at the same time will always be hard because of the interference.'

No matter how skilled we become and no matter how sophisticated the equipment at our disposal, there is a limit to the number of decisions per minute that we can take. In the case of a pilot it is crucial that this limit not be exceeded. Head-up displays, by which important visual information is placed directly in the pilot's line of sight, cut down on eye and head movements. Automation can also reduce cognitive overload: once the pilot has made a decision it is possible for him to press a button for certain tasks to be performed automatically thanks to the introduction of new instruments. But the limitations of the human brain and sensory apparatus must still be borne in mind.

Misguided 'improvements'

Attempts to improve cockpit design sometimes founder because of the designer's lack of first-hand flying experience. Wing-Commander Clive Rustin, who tests military aircraft for performance, safety and pilot

Above: the cockpit of a modern airliner. Below: Wing-Commander Clive Rustin.

comfort, gave us some graphic examples of efforts to ease the pilot's burden which went drastically wrong.

For example, to make it easier to adjust speed, an extra dial was added to the air-speed indicator of a commercial aircraft which showed the speed that would be achieved if no further adjustment was made. Similarly, an extra needle on the altimeter was supposed to simplify height adjustments. When these instruments were flight-tested individually they did indeed make it easier to adjust speed and height, but when added to the rest of the instrument panel they actually increased the workload of the pilot, who now had seven instruments to watch instead of five. 'It was a great *idea* in theory but it didn't work in reality,' says the Wing Commander.

When a military aircraft was superseded by a similar but more advanced model, Wing-Commander Rustin recalls, the designers reversed the positions of the rocket-firing button, which had previously been on the throttle, and the radio transmitter switch, which had been on the stick. This reversal had some dramatic consequences. On one occasion when a pilot was preparing to land, having forgotten to turn off his armament master switch, he pressed what he thought was his radio transmitter and fired two rockets. Air traffic control tried to inform him of what he had done but he did not hear the message properly. To ask for it to be repeated, he again pressed what he took to be the transmitter and promptly fired two more rockets.

After long, uneventful commercial flights combining cognitive overload, last-minute stress and sheer force of habit, pilots regularly land with their undercarriage retracted. Three green lights are illuminated in the cockpit when the undercarriage comes down, and the mandatory procedure for a pilot about to land is to call out 'Finals – three greens' when he has checked that the lights are on. Despite the simplicity of the procedure, over the years many pilots have automatically called out 'Finals – three greens' when in fact the wheels were still up. Trials to test additional ways of preventing this from happening have not been conclusive, according to Rustin, so the old system remains in use.

One suggestion has been a voice generator that tells the pilot 'Your wheels are not down' when he throttles back below a certain power setting. But there is a danger that such a device might simply contribute further to cognitive overload by making additional demands on the pilot's already overtaxed concentration.

The instant stress detector

This short personality test will tell you whether or not you are likely to become a victim of work stress. It has been extracted by Professor Cary Cooper of Manchester University from a much longer questionnaire on behaviour and heart disease.

For each of the eight questions below, tick whichever phrase in capital letters applies to you.

Are you CASUAL ABOUT APPOINTMENTS   or NEVER LATE?

Are you NOT COMPETITIVE   or VERY COMPETITIVE?

Are you A GOOD LISTENER   or DO YOU OFTEN INTERRUPT?

Are you NEVER RUSHED   or ALWAYS RUSHED?

Can you WAIT PATIENTLY   or are you IMPATIENT?

Do you usually EXPRESS YOUR FEELINGS   or do you tend to HIDE YOUR FEELINGS?

Do you TAKE THINGS ONE AT A TIME   or do you try to DO LOTS OF THINGS AT ONCE?

Are you EASY-GOING   or are you HARD-DRIVING?

If most of the ticks are in the boxes in the right-hand column, you exhibit what has become known as Type A behaviour (see 'Work-related Stress', p. 100): you are fairly impulsive, time-conscious, achievement-oriented and hard-driving. Because of these traits you are also more likely to suffer a heart attack and should think about slowing down. A majority of ticks in the left-hand boxes indicates Type B behaviour – you are more lethargic, less ambitious, more relaxed, and likely to live longer.

Interview

PROFESSOR PETER WARR, Director of the Social and Applied Psychology Unit at Sheffield University, who has spent many years investigating what it is that people get out of their jobs and what they miss most when they lose them, outlines to John Nicholson some of the hazards – and possible compensations – of unemployment.

JOHN NICHOLSON   First of all, what evidence is there that not having a job actually makes us ill?

PETER WARR   Let me first explain how we get this evidence. Over the past few years we've interviewed several thousand unemployed people in several parts of the country. We've compared their health and their experience of being unemployed with those of people in jobs; and we also followed people who've got jobs, seeing what happens to them when they lose their jobs, and sometimes seeing what happens when they become re-employed. These studies have revealed quite conclusively that being unemployed produces severe negative effects psychologically. These include increased anxiety, strain, worry, and symptoms of depression, like listlessness, apathy, turning in on yourself, and a general reduction in motivation. These symptoms usually disappear when people get work again.

JN   Have you found out what it is about work that we miss specifically?

PW   Well, it must be emphasized that people differ. But let me talk to begin with about the average effects. In general, I think that we can say that there are five main areas in which people are negatively affected when they become unemployed. First the question of money, obviously. Again, it's difficult to generalize, but let's say a half of your previous income, or maybe a little bit more, is what you get when you're unemployed. So that's a strain in itself.

The second problem is that you're no longer able to use the skills that you had before. There's a lot of pleasure associated with being skilful in your job; even simple-looking jobs need skills, and if a person is accomplished in working with those skills, it's very satisfying. You've got less chance to use those skills, less chance to develop new ones, and you may be feeling you're getting rusty when you become unemployed.

The third point is that you've got less pull from the environment, as it were. When you've got a job, you're required to get out of the house, to be in certain places at certain times, you've got responsibilities to other people. These responsibilities are reduced quite a lot when you become unemployed. You set yourself fewer personal objectives, and this is very important because psychological health in many ways depends upon having realistic objectives and attaining some of them.

Fourth is the fact that life generally is more threatening. You get your self-esteem battered in many ways when you're unemployed. You've got to apply for jobs when you know you've little chance of getting them, you've got to hassle over benefits, you've got to borrow money, you may have to struggle to repay that money. Life is insecure; you can't predict a future for yourself and your family. So the fourth point is increased threat and insecurity.

Fifth, I think we must emphasize the social psychological aspect of unemployment. And there are really two points here. You've got less social contact with people than you had – you don't see your workmates so much, you don't see so much of other people because you haven't got the money to go to the pub or whatever. You

Work is healthy! The hats being made by these psychiatric patients will be sold commercially, but the real purpose of the exercise is occupational therapy.

see less of people and you have fewer relationships. Also, your social position has been devalued: you've lost an important place in society. You see yourself as a second-class citizen, you've come down in the world. The social stigma of unemployment is really quite important.

JN You mention averages and individual differences. What sort of people are most affected by these?

PW That's very important. I'd like to start by talking about people in their thirties and forties, maybe family men with family responsibilities. There's no question at all that in psychological terms these are the people who suffer most in comparison with people of, say, fifty-five, sixty, who may be thinking of early retirement, and in comparison with teenagers. This is not to say that teenagers like to be unemployed – they don't, they desperately want to work – but in general the thirty- to forty-year-olds suffer particularly.

The second group that suffers a lot is the long-term unemployed people, and these people are becoming increasingly numerous. The worst

Unemployment can often liberate creative energy.

short-term psychological effects of unemployment level off after four to six months, but more than a million people in this country now have been out of work for a year or more. These are the people who are increasingly sensing that maybe they're not going to get a job again soon. Their motivation is reduced.

And thirdly, there are the people who are strong on the 'work ethic', which is central to our society at the moment. We've all of us been brought up to some degree to believe we should be working, that it's morally desirable to have a job. Some people feel this more than others, and the people who feel it most strongly, not surprisingly, are those who really suffer when they lose their jobs. The greater the commitment, the greater the distress.

In general, the working-class unemployed are affected worse than the middle class because they have less cash and fewer alternative activities to fall back on. Women who are the principal wage-earners in their family suffer as much as men, but mothers with young children seem to be much less affected psychologically.

JN That brings me to my last point: is there anybody who's actually happier without a job?

Long-term unemployment tends to sap morale.

PW Yes, I think so. Two kinds of people here again. First, people who've had very stressful jobs and are in a way glad to lose them. This could be because the working conditions were rotten or the job was physically hard or psychologically threatening. But the more interesting group, perhaps, consists of those who are coping well with unemployment because they've taken on work of a different kind. They're very actively involved in the Church, political groups, community groups, voluntary agencies, or they might be extending their education, or something of that kind. They're working hard, although they're not working within jobs, and that's psychologically healthy.

JN Is there anything we can learn from them about planning for the future?

PW Yes, unemployment doesn't have to be harmful. We have to face the fact that there are not going to be enough jobs to go round for the foreseeable future, whatever political party is in power. This is not a political point. We're not going to have enough full-time jobs, so we have to look at what sort of work people can do to keep themselves psychologically healthy. I certainly don't accept that we have a biological need to work. The need is actually socially constructed, and if we recognize this, there's no reason we shouldn't be able to reconstruct our ideas about work in such a way that not having a job loses its stigma and becomes socially acceptable.

Systime: An organizational success story

Systime is a computer company in Leeds started up by a husband and wife team determined to create a business less bureaucratic and less formal than the places in which they themselves had been employed. In ten years it has been so successful that it now has a staff of 1400.

All in the Mind visited Leeds to see how the company operates and to talk to the people who work there.

'We try to deal with people as individuals. We try to give them responsibility, to give them freedom to move and act . . . If you do that, you get an awful lot from them you get initiative, you get enthusiasm and you get excitement.'

These are the words of psychologist Steve Williams, who is the company's personnel manager. But just how does a large company go about creating this sense of *responsibility* and *freedom*?

In the case of Systime, employees are encouraged in numerous ways to be involved in their work and to feel that their contribution is valued. They *set their own pace*, depending on the amount of work to be done, and they work under *minimal supervision*. 'When there's no work to do, we can talk to people, walk around, discuss things,' says a young man who works as a packer. 'And when there's work to do you get on with it. There's no boss behind you all the time cracking the whip. And you get just as much work done, probably more.'

The fact that employees are organized into small teams creates a *group identity* and ready-made *support systems*, preventing the cog-in-a-wheel feeling that besets factory hands who work in psychological isolation. 'They all pull their weight and get the work out,' says Brenda, the supervisor of a section that makes printed-circuit boards, of the 25 women in her charge. Differences in levels of skill are acknowledged: the women who wire the circuit boards are paid slightly more than those who do the routine assembly work, but within the team every member plays a vital part and enjoys a sense of participation.

Not everyone, though, feels comfortable with this degree of autonomy. One recruit in three leaves within nine months of joining the company. But those who stay are enthusiastic in their praise. 'In my own experience,' says Steve Williams, 'coming here from a traditional engineering company was like having a ball and chain taken off my leg.'

PSYCHOLOGY IN ACTION

Top: Brenda, section supervisor (right), and a member of her team.
Centre: the restaurant.
Bottom: psychologist Professor Cary Cooper looks on as an employee answers a question for the computerized personality profile.

115

A *flat management structure* encourages informality and the exchange of ideas. There are only four levels between the chairman and the shopfloor, and everyone is on first-name terms. Management do not enjoy special parking or eating facilities. 'We don't believe in the sort of artificial hierarchies that you get in other British companies. Everybody here is of relatively equal status,' according to Steve Williams. He concedes that sometimes managers try to introduce the odd status symbol, such as wallpaper in their offices, but he hopes that it is just a matter of time before they change their attitudes.

Physical barriers are also kept to a minimum. The plant is laid out on an open plan so as to encourage communication between work groups. 'Ideally there would be no barriers between research and development on one side of the building and manufacturing on the other,' Steve Williams explains, adding that only fire regulations prevent this arrangement.

Because of the accent on communication, the company prides itself on being responsive to employees' complaints and suggestions. Steve Williams attributes the company's success to the fact that people are treated as individuals who have something to say about the jobs they do. Brenda, the printed-circuit boards supervisor, praises the management's willingness to listen to the complaints of the women in her section, which are elicited at regular 'moan sessions'.

Above: Steve Williams passes the friendly computerised security system on his arrival for work. Right: fetching and carrying is done by a robot, running along set routes and controlled by computer.

As an extension of the principle of making people feel they belong and are valued, a very attractive working environment has been created at Systime. There are troughs of pot plants throughout the building, and carpets where possible in the manufacturing area. The place is quiet and clean, and the restaurant, rather than being a dingy canteen, is a place to which employees bring their friends and families. 'The people I've brought round are quite amazed how nice it is,' says one worker. 'My mates think it's a bit of a holiday camp,' says another, referring to the relaxed atmosphere. 'It's not like a factory at all' is a remark that comes up constantly.

The lesson for other companies is spelled out by Steve Williams: 'If you treat people as I'm afraid a lot of industry in Britain does – as units to be moved here and there, as cogs in a wheel – then you get just that: a machine which is inflexible and just operates on automatic. If you treat people as responsible people able to give of their best, they respond in that way.'

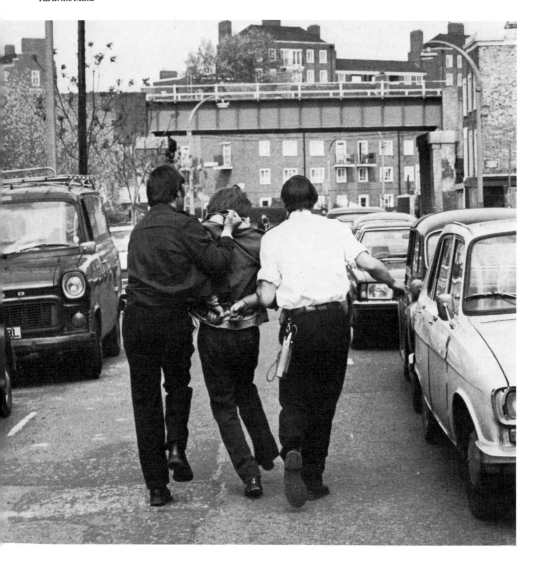

CRIME AND PUNISHMENT 6

Crime is still on the increase and it is clear that the standard approaches to understanding and preventing it are having little effect. Most people have fairly strong opinions as to the causes of crime: some believe that a person's upbringing decides whether he becomes a criminal or not; some believe that it is the situation in which a person finds himself that dictates whether or not he commits a crime; still others believe that criminals are 'born not made' and that 'once a criminal, always a criminal'. This last belief suggests that the criminal 'type' will never change. Which of these views is the more accurate? This question is not only of interest to psychologists; it is crucial to our decisions about how to reduce crime.

To test the accuracy of your views about crime and criminals, say if you agree with these statements. The correct answers are given at the end of this chapter.

1   The elderly run the greatest risk of being attacked.

2   Psychopaths are typically withdrawn and controlled.

3   Most victims of rape know their assailants.

4   Your chances of being robbed are lower than your chances of being admitted to hospital as a mental patient.

5   Most rapists are armed.

6   The typical householder must expect to be burgled every couple of years.

7   Young offenders under seventeen in Britain are responsible for less than 20 per cent of all crime.

8   Most crimes are not reported.

9   Anti-shoplifting signs increase shoplifting.

10 Once he's married, a man is likely to turn his back on crime.

Psychologists are now conducting research into the judicial process, into crime prevention and into the treatment of certain types of offenders. It is sometimes thought that information gained from studying people in prison will help us to reduce the incidence of crime. In fact this approach has a number of limitations: by no means everybody who commits a crime is caught and, unfortunately, not everybody in prison has actually committed an offence.

There have been several now notorious cases (as admitted in various government reports and inquiries) in which an innocent person has been wrongfully convicted and sent to prison on the basis of incorrect eyewitness testimony. Why do courts often accept mistaken identifications? One reason is that many people, including the police and jurors, are inclined to take more notice of what is said by a confident witness than by a hesitant, non-confident witness. Recent studies of eyewitnessing have found that there is no necessary relationship between how confident witnesses appear to be and the accuracy of their identifications. Another common belief is that fear or stress is likely to help a witness remember a face. In fact, the high fear or stress associated with a number of crimes is likely to lead to poorer remembering in witnesses. As a result of these findings, judges in Britain are now required to warn juries about the common fallibility of eyewitness evidence, and the police have become more careful about the way they question eyewitnesses so as not to introduce bias. As a result, the number of wrongful convictions based on this kind of evidence should decrease.

How reliable is eyewitness testimony? Placing the suspect in a line of people of similar appearance is just as likely to confuse the witness, who assumes that someone in the identity parade must be guilty.

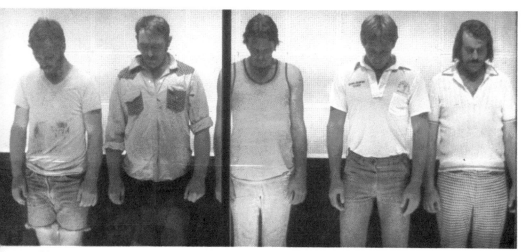

Other wrongful convictions occur because by no means all the people imprisoned as the result of a confession have in fact committed a crime. During police questioning people do confess to crimes which they did not commit. To find out why, psychologists have been conducting studies of interrogations and confessions. One of Britain's experts on this topic is Barrie Irving, who carried out research for the recent Royal Commission on Criminal Procedure. For a discussion of his findings, see 'We have ways . . .' on page 124

The issue of false confession highlights some of the problems facing the police when they have to decide whether a person is telling the truth or not. Research has shown that this is a very difficult thing to do: humans are not very good at deciding if someone is lying. But would a machine be any more accurate? A recent development in the USA has been the acceptance by the courts in some states of evidence based on the use of a polygraph (sometimes called a lie-detector). As yet, such evidence is not admissible in British courts, although polygraphs are to be used as part of the preliminary examination of people entering government security services. Psychologists have been examining the accuracy of these procedures. They conclude that if polygraphs were commonly used in attempts to determine whether police suspects were lying or not, their error rate would be too great to make them reliable, especially if used by the courts. However, the use of polygraphs in certain special cases may prove to be of value. For example, in a recent case of possible drunken driving, a man was breathalysed and asked to provide blood or urine samples. The man claimed to be a blood phobic. He said that he could not agree to provide a blood sample and that the anxiety aroused by this prospect made him unable to produce adequate urine samples. Later he was automatically convicted of drunken driving for refusing to provide blood or urine samples. Dr Gisli Gudjonsson, a psychologist at the Institute of Psychiatry in London, examined the man as part of his appeal against his conviction. Using the polygraph apparatus, Dr Gudjonsson was able to show that the man demonstrated a rapid and dramatic fall in blood pressure and heart rate when presented with blood samples or related objects. Since it is impossible to produce this response by voluntary action, Dr Gudjonsson proved to the appeal court's satisfaction that the man was indeed a genuine blood phobic. On the basis of this evidence the

The polygraph (lie-detector) being used by the FBI.

man was acquitted. This is the first time that such evidence has played a crucial role in a British court.

All the research mentioned so far has concerned events leading up to a person being convicted of a crime. It helps to explain why some of the people in prison should not, in fact, be there. This, and the fact that the majority of people who commit most types of crime are never caught, casts doubt on the assumption that the best way for us to understand crime is to study convicted criminals.

Furthermore, since crime is not, in fact, committed by a small minority of the population, the approach of 'us' studying 'them' may not necessarily lead to a reduction in crime. The recent British Crime Survey published by the Home Office suggests that by the age of 65 years, 45 per cent of males will have a criminal conviction.

Most people believe that the best way to reduce crime is to ensure that criminals are caught and punished, or caught and reformed. Psychologists believe that this may be rather unrealistic because research indicates that the best way to reduce crime would be to concentrate on prevention. Partly because of this research, the Home Office has now set up a special Crime Prevention Centre which will offer advice on how to reduce crime.

Many policing systems are based on the assumption that crime is committed by a distinct minority and this is perhaps one of the reasons why many such systems have turned out to be ineffective. For example, the patrolling of police officers in 'fast-response' cars has been found to waste time and money, and a recent survey showed that much crime is not even reported to the police.

Many psychologists try to understand crime as a particular kind of *decision-making process*. When an individual is in a position to commit a crime he will make a series of decisions concerning, for example, the degree of risk involved, the amount of reward, and how 'wrong' the crime is. These decisions will be influenced by a variety of factors, including the individual's mood and in particular his perceptions. However, the effects of these factors need to be considered within the context of the whole situation. As well as determining how decision-making processes operate, psychologists have been examining the situations in which crime takes place. They can help to design or alter environments in order to reduce the opportunity for crime, for instance in the planning of houses and housing estates, so that each house or flat has a 'defensible space' against crime.

In this way the incidence of a variety of frequent crimes that the police are finding it extremely difficult to cope with – for instance, burglary – can be substantially reduced. Psychologists argue that the most effective deterrent is the *likelihood of being caught* (even if the resulting punishment is minor) rather than the size of the punishment.

It is the likelihood of being caught that is the deterrent: (left) a criminal on his way to court hides his identity under a blanket; (right) a bank raid captured on film.

The emphasis that psychologists are now putting on the way that criminals perceive the world is also bearing fruit with juvenile offenders, most of whom have committed minor crimes. It is now widely accepted that the present penal system fails to change people so that they do not re-offend. If psychologists are claiming that they are beginning to find out why people commit crime, can they come up with any alternatives to imprisonment? Can they offer anything which would help to prevent young offenders from setting out on an inevitable life of crime?

Research has shown that traditional forms of treatment are typically ineffective when it comes to changing people's behaviour in a positive way. They have rarely been concerned with the possibility that people commit offences partly as a result of their perceptions and beliefs in a specific situation rather than as a reflection of enduring personality traits. Professor Norman Tutt of Lancaster University has been involved in the setting up of new procedures in the detention centres where juvenile offenders are often sent. He believes they can be taught to understand and control the elements in a situation which facilitate their committing an offence. For a closer look at his methods in action at an intermediate treatment centre, see Psychology in Action, page 137.

We have ways...

Under British law, a person is deemed innocent unless proved guilty. For this reason, it is generally assumed, and often repeated, that an innocent person has nothing to fear from the law. But in fact ordinary, innocent people often confess to offences they have not committed. Why should this be so?

When in police custody, a suspect is often locked away, with no knowledge of what is going on outside the room. Any information he receives is controlled by the interrogator. In this situation he may be more impressed by the short-term advantages of getting out of the room than the long-term consequences of falsely confessing and, whether he is aware of doing it or not, the interrogator is able to manipulate the suspect. The police aim is to get suspects to cooperate, but there is a danger that particular techniques, when used on people with particular characteristics such as low IQ or low self-esteem, may actually distort the truth.

Thanks to the work of psychologists, there is a growing official awareness of the influence of interrogation techniques. Training programmes for police officers are now stressing the importance of understanding the effects of styles of questioning. In the courts, judges now try to determine whether the techniques used in an interrogation may have made a confession unreliable.

Psychologist Barrie Irving has been investigating police interrogation methods for the Royal Commission on Criminal Procedure. From his research in police stations he has identified four main strategies – which we shall refer to as methods A, B, C and D – used by the police to influence the decision-making of suspects.

Barrie Irving (left) with actor Michael Carter who plays the police officer in the interrogation scenes in the T.V. programme.

Each method has a slightly different purpose:

Method A plays up the advantages of admission

Method B plays down the advantages of denial

Method C plays down the drawbacks of admission

Method D plays up the drawbacks of denial

Here is what each of the methods might sound like, although in practice the distinctions may not be so clear-cut:

Method A: 'Be a man'
I understand that it requires a lot of courage to admit to something like this, but I think you've got the courage and the strength to take it. I know at the moment you're probably as low as you've ever been in your life. Well, you get this off your chest, you've no idea how much better you're going to feel. Think of the value it's going to have for your family. If they see that you've got the courage to stand up, face the music and admit to this, you're going to rise in their estimation. You plead guilty, it'll all be over and done with in no time at all and you can go home. We'll hear your side of the story and you never know, it might not even reach the court.

The 'soft' interview (methods A and C) with a 'sympathetic' and 'reasonable' officer.

Method B: 'It's pointless denying it'
Still insist on denying this? We've got all the evidence we need. We wouldn't have gone to the trouble of arresting you if we didn't have the evidence to convict you. You're going to be charged with it anyway. It's useless for you to deny it because I can see that you're lying. I've been in this situation hundreds of times before. Anybody could walk into this room and see right through you. Anyway, your mate's made a full statement.

Method C: 'There's no need to be afraid'
Now the law says that the courts are going to have to have a very good reason to send first offenders to prison. If we hear your side of the story, it may not even get to court. I mean, this kind of thing goes on a lot. It's hardly the Crown Jewels, is it? Anyway, there's quite a bit of waste in your company, things left lying around. Anything you say will be treated in the strictest confidence. There's no way that we're going to say that

you shopped anybody or anything like that. It's not as if you're a criminal, but obviously you do need some help. And as for your wife, well of course she's going to forgive you.

Method D: 'You'll be sorry'

It's a simple, straightforward case. You're going to drag it out and make it complicated. It means that we're going to have to go back down to your place of work to make a few more enquiries, and you know what that means. It means that more of your mates are going to know what you've been up to. Think of the effect it's going to have on your family. Haven't you put them through enough already? And this idiotic alibi your wife's come up with . . . I can't blame her – she's totally right to stand by you. Of course she is. But when we convict you, what does that make her? An accessory, that's what.

The dangers of manipulation

Barrie Irving found that policemen who had not been properly trained in the questioning of suspects had nevertheless intuitively developed sophisticated techniques. They tended to favour methods B and D, which concentrate on the consequences of denial, as opposed to the 'softer' methods A and C, which stress the consequences of admission. In method D, which is the 'hardest' of all, the detective tries to make it impossible for the suspect to deny the offence. His aim is to increase the suspect's fear that if he continues with his denial things will get very much worse, not better, whereas the suspect has probably been behaving on the assumption that if he simply keeps quiet all will be well.

Barrie Irving believes interrogation is a legitimate strategy for police to use, given that it is an important part of the criminal process. He is quick to point out, however, that methods B and D present certain dangers. They may elicit false confessions and may adversely affect suspects who are easily suggestible, especially when they are used by inexperienced officers who may not be conscious of what they are doing.

Gisli Gudjonsson notes that his own research and that of others show that some people are unexpectedly suggestible. 'It's clear, for instance, that you can get people to give in to leading questions and, more importantly, to questions that are not necessarily

leading but somehow misleading.' Suspects who do not understand the pros and cons of what they are doing may be offered false alternatives and make a choice simply because they think they ought to give an answer. When faced with negative feedback, as in methods B and D, the suspect is effectively being told that his evidence isn't good enough, that he is not believed, and that he should come up with a better story. He may do just that.

Police statements, says Gudjonsson, are in effect a compromise, a bargaining process. The person is being interrogated in order to give the information that the police officer wants to hear, but the truth may recede in the process. 'The more police officers feed people with information, the more they keep repeating certain questions and certain salient facts, the more these facts become incorporated into people's memories. Even though they're not aware of this at the time, weeks later this information becomes a part of their own memory collection and they may firmly believe it to be true, even though it was introduced to them by the police in the first instance.'

Arthur Miller's play The Crucible *about witch-hunts in Salem, Massachusetts, has several scenes, including a famous court scene, in which the young witnesses' testimony is expertly manipulated.*

The 'hard' technique (methods B and D) with a 'tough' officer.

Of course, some cases of false testimony are deliberate lies, but others are the result of susceptibility on the part of the suspect combined with the effects of interrogation techniques. Poor self-esteem, low intelligence and a poor memory are three factors highly correlated with suggestibility.

Textbooks of interrogation techniques, Gudjonsson points out, stress the need for the officer to maximise the distance between himself and the suspect by tightly controlling the interrogation context (for instance, by keeping the suspect in physical and psychological isolation), by trying to induce anxiety and guilt, and by appearing confident and competent. 'Even though you can get more information by using these techniques, you may make some people particularly susceptible to giving wrong testimony because you are manipulating their poor self-esteem or their vulnerabilities.'

Protecting the innocent

'We all use persuasive techniques in talking to each other,' says Barrie Irving, 'and we are the targets of persuasive techniques when we listen to advertising or to politicians.' But in view of the fact that many policemen find it hard to believe that their techniques could be so effective as to elicit false confessions, and in view of the important consideration that a suspect has no freedom of choice or movement, there is a need for clear-cut guidelines and safeguards covering interrogation techniques. 'Any technique can become oppressive if it's used to excess.'

Barrie Irving's report is already having far-reaching effects. Detective training courses are being improved to take an analytical look at interrogation techniques, so that policemen can become aware – with the help of video – of how they are operating and where they should draw the line. By way of external controls, the Home Office is producing a code of conduct governing interrogations.

Given the greater awareness throughout the judicial system, and these safeguards, we might hope for a gradual drop in the number of convictions based on false confessions.

Fit the face to the crime

Given a list of crimes and a series of photographs, most people have little difficulty in matching the two, and there is wide agreement as to who did what. Try this test for yourself. Look carefully at the six photographs above, then examine the following list of offences:

Soliciting

Illegal possession of drugs

Grievous bodily harm

Arson

Fraud

Taking and driving away

Armed robbery

Now fit the face to the crime. For each photograph decide which offence the person has committed.

Psychologist Ray Bull of the North East London Polytechnic conducted this experiment with the *All in the Mind* studio audience. It is similar to large-scale experiments he has conducted to see whether or not

129

people do share common beliefs about which face fits which crime.

The reactions of the studio audience were similar to those of the people in the larger-scale experiments. Looking at the photographs of the men, people thought they saw perpetrators of grievous bodily harm, illegal possession of drugs and soliciting. The women in the photographs were identified as perpetrators of fraud, illegal possession of drugs and armed robbery.

In fact the studio participants were all wrong. The people in these photographs are all students who have not committed any of the offences listed.

Ray Bull's findings have shown that we expect criminals to be unattractive, ugly, nasty and 'criminal-looking'. Thus, a jury is more likely to be convinced of someone's guilt if the person being tried is unattractive than if they are nice-looking. And they actually require less evidence before convicting. Nor is it only the juries which are influenced in this way: the police and magistrates, too, expect criminals to be ugly, Ray Bull has discovered.

Ray Bull

The same bias is shown in identification parades: 'Witnesses often tend to pick out the ugliest, most "criminal-looking" type in the parade even if he is only a passer-by that the police have asked to take part,' says Ray Bull.

However, the fact that people are only too eager to jump to wrong conclusions does not mean that there is no relationship at all between crime and physical appearance. Ray Bull's work shows that members of the public share common beliefs about what constitutes a criminal appearance, and there is some evidence that these beliefs may actually play a part in causing criminality. For instance, a child's looks are known to influence adults' judgements of misbehaviour. In experiments, both experienced teachers and inexperienced students were more likely, on the basis of written reports and photographs, to recommend leniency for an attractive child than an unattractive one. They were likely to regard a misdemeanour in an attractive child as a temporary aberration, and to construe the same offence in an unattractive child as anti-social behaviour requiring severe punishment.

If the stereotype correlating ugliness with bad character is in operation even when a child is of nursery school age, it is not hard to see how an unattractive appearance might actually contribute to a future of deviancy.

Interview

The notion that criminals are a race apart lingers on in the public imagination even though theories linking crime and character have achieved little of practical value. John Nicholson put the question 'Is there a criminal personality?' to two prominent psychologists at work in widely differing settings. In both cases the answer is a qualified 'no'. DR RON CLARKE (above) of the Home Office goes on to put the case for altering the environment as a means of crime prevention, while TONY BLACK (below), head of the Psychology Department at Broadmoor Hospital, welcomes new ways of assessing the progress of dangerous offenders.

JOHN NICHOLSON Do you think that criminals are different from the rest of us?

RON CLARKE Well, some criminals are different, but a great deal of crime is actually committed by fairly ordinary people acting under temptation, given certain opportunities. Anyone can commit a crime given the right circumstances and right motivation.

JN So, do you believe that there is any such thing as a criminal personality?

RC I think that some people have what might be called a criminal personality, but they are in the minority. Where people commit very serious sexual crimes or psychopathic murders, obviously personality factors are very important. But I doubt very much that, for the great run of crime, there is a particular personality that predisposes you to commit a particular offence.

Myra Hindley

Dennis Nilsen

Reggie Kray

Ronald Biggs

JN Is there any specific treatment of criminals that really works?

RC A great deal of research has been done into the effectiveness of different forms of treatment for offenders. There's been research into different forms of institutional treatment, different forms of non-institutional treatment – probation, social work, therapeutic community type methods. All these have been tried but none seems to work terribly well. It's difficult to be very precise about how well these treatments work, because it's hard to know what would happen if they weren't applied. Generally speaking, you have to compare treatments of different kinds and see whether one works better than the other. And the message of many hundreds of research studies is that no one treatment is really much better than any other.

JN On this question of treatment, is it the case that short, swingeing, more punishing sentences are the answer? Does deterrence work at all?

RC The evidence on deterrence shows that the more important factor is certainty of getting caught, rather than how severely someone is dealt with when they *are* caught. A lot of people at the point of committing a crime are not really thinking about the consequences of what might happen if they're caught. They're more likely to be thinking, am I going to get caught? That is the point to remember about deterrence.

JN Perhaps more policemen on the beat might be the answer?

RC The police are faced with a very difficult set of problems in trying to do anything about crime. Crime is usually committed at a time and place of the offender's choosing. This makes it very difficult for the police to be where they should be if they're actually going to prevent crime through patrolling. The other main type

of police activity is detective work. But many research studies have shown that it's difficult for the police actually to solve the crime unless they have a very good idea from the victim or witnesses who has committed the offence. They can spend an awful lot of time looking for clues that just are not there.

JN So, what in your view is the best way to reduce crime?

RC The most important thing when thinking about reducing crime is to talk very specifically about certain types of offences. Crime is a collection of a whole set of different behaviours. You need to split crime up into its different constituents and then think carefully about what are the circumstances that gave rise to that particular type of offence. And then, when you've done that, think carefully about whether there are things you could do to manipulate those circumstances. Generally speaking, these boil down to seeing whether you can increase the certainty of getting caught if a crime is contemplated or committed, or else simply reducing the physical opportunities. On the basis of looking at a very wide range of research, environmental manipulation seems to me to be the most promising way of preventing or reducing crime.

JN Tony Black, first of all, do you think Broadmoor inmates are too bizarre to tell us anything about crime in the normal population?

TONY BLACK I don't think Broadmoor patients are too bizarre. Extreme variations of human behaviour can tell you something about the less extreme variations that other people have to deal with.

JN Do you believe in such a thing as a criminal personality, or do different types of crime and offender perhaps have different personalities to go with them?

TB I don't think there is a criminal personality as such. However, there are lots of different interacting personality factors that can load a person's disposition towards behaving criminally.

JN Can you give us some examples of specific types of crime being linked with different sorts of personality?

TB The only form of personality type clearly associated with criminal behaviour is the so-called psychopathic personality, who is, almost by definition, a person who behaves anti-socially, which makes it a circular definition. But this type is nevertheless based on certain temperamental, cognitive and physiological differences which dispose a person towards anti-social behaviour.

JN Is there such a thing as a typical murderer?

TB Murderers are interesting because, as a group, they have a much larger proportion of a personality type which is quite the opposite of the psychopathic personality: a very withdrawn, controlled type of personality, the opposite of the outgoing, impulsive, uncontrolled psychopathic type.

JN Is it the case, as many people fear, that Broadmoor patients are really too dangerous ever to be released?

Tony Black and colleagues at a Broadmoor staff meeting.

TB   When they arrive Broadmoor patients are obviously too dangerous to release – that's why they're there. That's what special hospitals exist for. When they're discharged, they're reckoned, to the best of our accumulated technical knowledge, not to be dangerous.

JN   Can you just give us some examples of how it is decided that someone is ready to be released from Broadmoor?

TB   Decisions that people are ready for release are arrived at by the clinical team as a whole, so that you're combining the expertise of a lot of different professional disciplines. The psychologist's contribution is the assessment of various personality traits, behavioural styles, dispositions and situational factors which the patient may be vulnerable to and assessing those factors in conjunction with the changes that have taken place since the patient arrived.

JN   Talking of change, on the basis of your research and experience, how optimistic are you about the possibility of people changing themselves, or being changed?

TB   It's an interesting question how far people are fundamentally able to change. I think that probably most changes are only ever fairly superficial. But to the extent that you can help people change their behaviour and control it and adopt different ways of tackling stressful life situations, you can improve and change their strategies for dealing with life. You perhaps haven't changed their fundamental personality; you've changed their strategies of behaviour.

JN   People may find what you say about assessing when people are ready to leave Broadmoor worryingly vague. Isn't there some sort of biological or even biochemical technique that could be used that's more precise?

TB Well, it's true that in assessing readiness for discharge, most of the procedures currently used are based on statistical distributions of a particular feature in the population. But techniques are coming along that are based on the physiological state – the usual physiological reactions to stress, like blood pressure changes, breathing changes, skin resistance changes – and there are other more biochemical methods coming along which look hopeful. We may be on the way to something that will extend the purely psychological approaches based on statistical inferences.

JN You work in a place where people have been institutionalized. Do you ever have the feeling that you can't really help them there, that they have to get out into the real world again?

TB I often have the feeling that the treatment can't be completed without their getting into the outside world, because you can only carry through a certain amount of the treatment in an institution. If you're dealing with people whose problems lie in their interactions with their fellow men and women, their families, in the real world, under stress of work, exposed to the normal social pressures (drink, for instance) you can't complete treatment in a closed, artificial institution. You've got to be able to move people through a progression of treatment environments, until ultimately they come out at the other end into a free and independent world.

JN Finally, is there any way to be certain of zero recidivism?

TB The only way you can be certain of zero recidivism is not to let anyone out, and if that happens you'll need to build a new Broadmoor about every five years. You'd also, as we know from our follow-up studies, be keeping lots of people in an institution who don't need to be there, and you'd thus be offending all our philosphical principles of individual liberty.

Focus on intermediate treatment

Millions of pounds are spent each year on attempts to rehabilitate young offenders under seventeen, who are responsible for 36 per cent of all crime. Yet eight out of ten of the offenders leaving Borstal or youth custody commit another offence within two years.

PSYCHOLOGY IN ACTION

One of the few rays of hope in this generally dismal picture is the relative success of community-based day-care centres. These centres offer intermediate treatment to young people considered to be at risk as well as to young persistent offenders. So-called intermediate treatment is far cheaper than residential care yet may be more effective in preventing young people from going back to their criminal ways. The thinking behind it is that it is far less damaging (and less expensive) not to take juvenile offenders into custody. 'What you see in Borstal or residential establishments for dealing with offenders is a concentration of delinquent attitudes,' says Norman Tutt, a former Civil Service psychologist who is now Professor of Applied Social Studies at Lancaster University. 'If you put a small group of people together, all with the same attitude, what you do is strengthen those attitudes, particularly if you cut them off from other contact.'

Professor Norman Tutt

Intermediate treatment centres provide a valuable location in which to try out a new type of treatment which Professor Tutt has helped to develop, and like most successful applications of psychological research, it is based not on some grand theory of human motivation but on the fine-grained analysis of how real people behave in specific circumstances. It tailors the treatment to the specific offence and aims to show that it is possible to change offenders' attitudes by offering them alternative styles of behaviour, so that they have the choice of opting out of delinquency.

The majority of male adolescents break the law at least once. But once they are caught and become involved in the penal system, their identity as offenders is reinforced. Intermediate treatment deals with the problem at several levels. Unlike, say, therapeutic communities, in which only the beliefs of the offender are examined, or Outward Bound schemes, which seek to change offenders by changing their environment, the new centres aim to change the offender's attitudes, by showing them new kinds of behaviour and social skills.

Redlees is a new day centre in Middlesex which offers

137

intermediate treatment to some fifty young offenders a year. Its director, Margery Rooke, observes that in the past, intermediate treatment for offenders has often involved 'compensatory activity' based on the idea that delinquency is a product of deprivation. She has personal reservations about the kind of thinking that resulted in young offenders being taken on rock-climbing or pony-trekking excursions. 'I began to think that we ought to provide something that was more related to the offence.'

Thus, in a twelve-week programme, boys (it is rare for a girl to be sent to Redlees) are helped to understand the nature of their crimes and their own motivation. 'We assume that they don't want to commit offences . . . We think that kids don't actually like going to court, spending the night in police cells, being expelled from school. They may well continue that behaviour, but they don't actually enjoy it.'

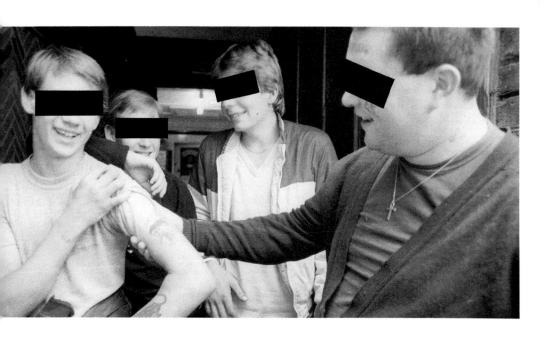

Redlees

Eight to ten boys attend at any one time, working as a group but remaining the responsibility of their parents when not at the centre. Each offender follows a set procedure: the first step, the assessment, involves filling out cards asking questions about past offences, giving details of date, time, place, accomplices and so on. Attention is then focused on one offence of particular

significance to the boy. He is asked to draw it in strip cartoon form and to present it to the rest of the group, who are free to question him or comment. The strip cartoon is then dramatized by the group (the offender whose story it is may direct or take a role), recorded on videotape and played back. The offender is then invited to discuss the tape, viewing his experience from the outside, and to consider alternative courses of action he might have taken at various stages. The final stage is for the whole group to continue role-playing, changing roles and exploring alternative behaviour.

The case of 'Jack', a fourteen-year-old who since the age of eleven has been convicted of several offences including burglary, gives a good illustration of what young offenders stand to gain from Redlees. Like most young offenders, Jack had only a hazy notion of what his sentence entailed. 'It was, you know, cleared out. Nobody said nothing about it and I just went,' he tells Margery Rooke when asked to give details about the outcome of his court appearance. He remains vague even when it is pointed out to him that he must have received a sentence ('Oh, he said it was nothing') and only after Margery Rooke's further suggestion that he was probably given a conditional discharge does he agree: 'Two years, something like that.' This characteristic confusion over sentencing, says Margery Rooke, indicates that the judicial process is not having the desired effect. 'It isn't actually creating a feeling for them that they have been punished.' At Redlees, boys are asked for full details of all their offences and sentences, their records are checked, and they are helped to understand the nature of their sentence.

One of the purposes of depicting the story of an offence in strip cartoon form is the opportunity it gives to identify what are known as *stop points* – those moments at which critical decisions are made. 'We're trying to get the kids to recognize that life is a series of decisions and that what you have to do is make the appropriate decision at any given time,' says Margery Rooke. With the help of the group, Jack recognizes several such points in his account of the burglary he has chosen to focus on: swearing at his mother; going to call for his friend Tony; suggesting that they do 'something bad'; deciding to rob the house; deciding to gain entry through the open window.

Once the stop points have been identified, it is easier for Jack to see how he could have behaved differently. Role-playing gives him a chance to explore alternative

Jack draws a strip cartoon to illustrate an offence he committed.

behaviour. For instance, the scene with his mother (Jack leaves the house after swearing at his mother, who has accidentally spilled coffee over him) may first be enacted with Jack playing himself and Margery Rooke playing his mother. After a group discussion about how this scene could have been handled differently, they might switch roles and introduce a different ending: in this particular case, instead of flying off the handle, Jack simply chose to go into the kitchen to fetch a cloth and wipe up the spilled coffee. Margery Rooke believes that such rehearsals of alternative responses allow the offenders to opt out of delinquency. 'This is the real learning point,' she says.

Delinquents characteristically fail to consider the possible consequences of their actions. Jack is no exception. 'It didn't cross my mind at the time,' he says when asked by one of the group if he had thought what might happen if he was caught. But by the end of one of the role-playing exercises exploring alternative behaviour, Jack has learned two lessons that will be very valuable to him in the outside world: he has learned to say no (to a boy who is playing the part of his accomplice, Tony, and who is trying to persuade him to go for a ride on a stolen motorbike) and he has learned to consider the implications of his acts.

TONY	Come on, we'll go out on my bike.
JACK	No, last time you done that I got into trouble, didn't I?
TONY	We'll go shooting then.
JACK	No.
TONY	Why not?
JACK	Ain't worth it.

Learning to refuse is no mean feat: it entails denying himself something he greatly enjoys (riding bikes), he risks offending his friend, being branded a goody-goody, and possibly feeling left out – all important considerations in adolescence, when peer groups, conforming, image and personal identity are vital issues. Jack is able to admit: 'Felt like I was being really horrible to him. I wanted to say yeah, but something inside said, no, don't in case you get caught.'

Recognizing painful feelings such as these is all part of the treatment at Redlees. Although the methods used – videos, cartoons and so on – are designed to engage the boys' attention and get them involved in what they are

learning, the lessons themselves are far from being fun. 'Kids often find it very difficult to talk about offences where they behaved badly. They do feel guilty, even though they don't appear to and are often very ashamed about some of the things they've done. To have to stand up in a group of people and actually talk about why they did it and so on is not an easy experience,' Margery Rooke emphasizes. In the course of cartoon and role-playing exercises Jack acknowledges that he felt 'quite bad' when he swore at his mother, that he was angry when he decided to call for Tony, that he was bored when he suggested doing 'something bad', and that he wouldn't have had the courage to rob the house if Tony hadn't been with him. (However, he rejects the suggestion that he was showing off in front of Tony.)

All these feelings have played their part in motivating Jack to commit his offence. By becoming conscious of them he has a better chance of changing the sequence in the future. Margery Rooke believes one of the unique strengths of the sort of treatment offered at Redlees is that it attempts to get offenders to understand the motivating factors behind their behaviour. 'When children are sentenced to periods of detention, they do all kinds of fairly difficult activities, but at no point does anybody ask them or talk to them about the particular offence that they've committed.'

A stint at Redlees confers further benefits. Instead of having his negative attitudes strengthened, Jack is learning to relate to his peers in a positive way, contributing to their search for understanding, giving and receiving suggestions, cooperating and sharing. In the process he often acquires a better self-image, learning to think of himself as a person who has a choice in life.

So how effective is Redlees? Margery Rooke says it is too early to draw definite conclusions because a two-year follow-up is required and the centre has not yet been in operation that long. But a few things are certain: although attendance is voluntary, the attendance rate is 'amazing'; no child has committed an offence while attending the centre; and thanks to supportive after-care, offences committed later are much less serious. All this is achieved at relatively little expense. Whereas it can cost the taxpayer up to £600 per week to keep a young offender in a residential centre, at centres like Redlees far more promising results are being achieved at a fraction of the cost.

Top: Jack's story is acted out in front of video cameras. Bottom: Margery Rooke suggests alternative ways of behaving in the same situation.

141

Answers to quiz on page 119.

1 False. Old people are the least frequent victims of violent crime; the most frequent victims are young men.

2 False. The psychopath is characteristically outgoing, impulsive and uncontrolled.

3 True.

4 True.

5 False. Thirty per cent are armed.

6 False. Houses are burgled less often than they catch fire.

7 False. The true figure is 36 per cent.

8 True.

9 True.

10 True and false. A tricky one, this. Getting married reduces criminality among men in their twenties, but those men who do continue their criminal activities after marrying actually commit more crimes than before.

ANXIETY

Edvard Munch's painting,
Anxiety.

Feeling anxious is an experience we share not just with
every member of the human race but with all living
creatures. The reason for this is very simple. Worrying
is not just a bad habit we ought to be trying to cure; on
the contrary, it is literally a life-saver because it is what
stops us running out into a busy street, just as it stopped
our ancestors from wandering into unexplored caves
and being snapped up by lurking predators. At less
intense levels, anxiety has great value, in that worrying
about the consequences of our actions prevents us doing
things we might later regret. In time of crisis, it is worry
that makes us face, and perhaps find a solution to,
whatever problem is making us anxious. And in less
extreme circumstances, mild anxiety gees us up to
perform more effectively, at work or sport, for example.

But although anxiety may be necessary, it is rarely
enjoyable, and never in its extreme manifestations,

when it can give rise to the various forms of neurotic behaviour which clinical psychologists spend much of their time helping people to understand and modify. Although it is human anxiety that concerns us, the discovery of why we feel acute anxiety and how the brain registers this state calls for detailed physiological investigation which cannot be carried out on human subjects. However, emotional behaviour (that is, all actions designed either to avoid pain or achieve pleasure) is under the control of brain structures that are strikingly similar in all mammals – unlike some other areas of the brain. And although many people are offended by the practice of carrying out experiments on live animals, it must be said that we owe some of our most important insights into human emotional behaviour – and most of the drugs used to alleviate anxiety – to studies of the laboratory rat.

Laboratory experiments confirm what common sense tells us – that anxiety is a response to the experience of threat. Dr Jeffrey Gray, who heads the Department of Psychology at the Institute of Psychiatry in London, has designed a series of experiments showing that what we call anxiety is actually the reaction of specific parts of the brain – both in rats and human beings – to any sort of threat, whether physical or psychological. What is interesting about these experiments, apart from their practical significance, is that they demonstrate that not getting a reward that is expected – what the layman calls frustration or disappointment and the psychologist calls frustrative non-reward – acts as a punishment in that it produces the same brain responses and behaviour as does pain. Anxiety is evoked not by punishment or frustration as such but by the *threat* of these events.

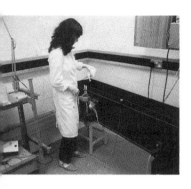

A laboratory rat in a simple runway in search of a 'reward', usually food.

Rats which learn that they will be given a tasty snack if they press a bar while a light is flashing soon come to associate the light itself with the reward of food. Since the rats press the bar more and more often, psychologists know they must find the experience rewarding. This is classical, Pavlovian conditioning, which forms the basis of hosts of psychological experiments in such fields as learning, emotion and personality (*see* Chapter 1).

In the same way, a rat can be trained to expect food when it reaches the box at the end of a simple runway. At first its movements will be slow and tentative, but with repeated trials, the fact that it comes to move much faster clearly indicates that it has built up an expectation of reward. This learning is an essential first step towards understanding how that rat will respond to anxiety.

Once the rat has come to expect the reward, the absence of food at the end of the runway changes its behaviour. The rat acts as though it is being punished or given a painful shock. For example, if there is another rat in an empty box in which neither rat has ever found food, the two animals will behave in a friendly way towards each other. But if one of the rats expected food there and does not find it, it often attacks the other rat. Frustration, then, can clearly lead to aggression.

Pain also reliably produces aggression. But Dr Gray has demonstrated, through the use of drugs in animal experiments, that the brain mechanism which mediates pain is distinct from the mechanism mediating anxiety. In other words, the threat of an unpleasant occurrence and an actual unpleasant occurrence (e.g. punishment, failure, frustration) engage different parts of the brain.

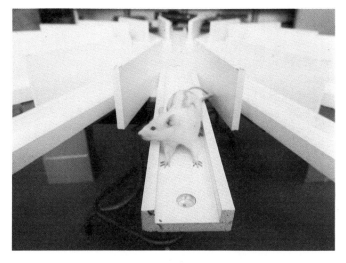

A rat in a more complicated environment – a maze.

Using this physiological analysis of anxiety and the concepts of reward and punishment, it becomes possible to investigate the reasons why some people are more susceptible than others to anxiety and to behavioural disorders in which anxiety is a prominent feature, for instance phobias or obsessive-compulsive neuroses. Recent research, according to Dr Gray, confirms that such anxiety-prone individuals – as would be expected – are particularly sensitive to threat (that is, to stimuli associated with punishment or frustration) but relatively insensitive to stimuli associated with reward. This discovery has interesting implications and may in time open up new or complementary approaches to the treatment of anxiety.

145

Interview

Dr Jeffrey Gray expands on his work and its practical significance in an interview with John Nicholson.

JOHN NICHOLSON Could I ask you first a question that I know many people would like an answer to: is it really necessary to make animals suffer in order to understand human anxiety?

JEFFREY GRAY Well, 'suffer', of course, is a loaded word. In most psychological experiments, in fact, very little is done that could make an animal suffer. Even when one is studying stress, one keeps the level of suffering as low as possible. If one uses even a painful stimulus, it's typically of the kind that a pet owner might inflict on a dog, say, with a rolled up newspaper, and in many experiments we deliberately use the non-delivery of an expected reward, because this produces very similar effects to a painful event.

JN Is anxiety for the rat really the same as anxiety for human beings?

JG I think essentially it is, and we've good evidence for that claim. The first piece of evidence is that anxiety is a response to threat. We've seen in experiments how this operates in animals, and common sense tells us that it is true of people. The other evidence we have that anxiety is essentially the same in animals as in man is that the drugs which are used to control anxiety, such as Valium, act upon specialized receptors in the brain, and these receptors are exactly the same in all mammals besides our own species. So we've very good evidence that not only the psychology but also the physiology of anxiety is the same.

JN What actually are the symptoms of anxiety that are common?

JG In the body, the heart is pounding, the pulse is thunderous, there is a release of adrenalin from the adrenal glands. Much more interesting, however, is what's going on in the brain, because that's what really underlies anxiety. The evidence we have is that critical structures in the limbic system are very active during anxiety. These are structures such as the hippocampus and the amygdala, which are under the control of long nerve-fibres that start in the brainstem. These long nerve-fibres act as a kind of alarm system for the brain, alerting the whole of the forebrain, including the hippocampus and the amygdala, but also structures such as the neocortex, which are more advanced in man.

JN What are the most important practical spin-offs of this sort of research?

JG There are many things one could point to, but perhaps I could emphasize just two areas of research. One is that if you repeatedly expose an animal such as a rat to something that makes it anxious, for example a stimulus associated with a mild electric shock or with frustration, the animal toughens up and becomes much more

Prolonged exposure to stressful situations 'toughens' the mind and enables people to cope with situations which they would previously have found too difficult. Coping with the horrors of war is an extreme example of this process in action.

able to resist disruption from these events. One of the things we've been working on is the brain mechanisms which underlie this toughening-up process. We've shown how these brain mechanisms are affected by the drugs that people use to control anxiety. What we've found is a little alarming from the point of view of a drug user. If we subject an animal to a series of experiences that would normally cause it to become more resistant to stress, but at the same time inject it with Valium or Librium, we find that the drug, even though it reduces its immediate level of anxiety, prevents this development of spontaneous toughening up, which has implications for the drug user.

JN We've seen that anxiety is similar in man and animals. Is it the same for different people?

JG No, certainly not. Both in animals and in people there are clearly considerable differences between individuals in their susceptibility to anxiety. In the rat, for example, there are important genetic factors; some strains of rats are much more fearful than others, and the same is true of people. There are also differences due to experience. If you've had a lot of stress in your life, you can go one way or the other. Some people become more and more sensitive to stress, others become much more tolerant of stress, but all of these differences in the end, I feel sure, have to funnel through the brain, and that's why we're working on the brain.

Dr Gray injecting a laboratory rat with Valium to test its action on the animal's brain and behaviour.

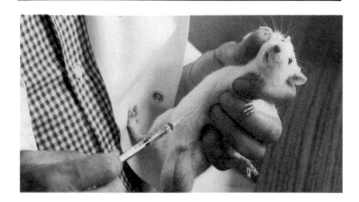

Worrying

It is often assumed that worrying is a product of modern urban society, and anxiety has been labelled the official emotion of our age. It is an attractive idea that if we could only turn the clock back to some unspecified Golden Age, our worries would disappear. But a look at the causes of our worries will soon make it clear that no period in the past was any less worrying than the present; indeed it may have been more so.

It is not easy to assess accurately the amount of mental illness people suffer today, let alone in the past, but in 1773 an English doctor calculated that nervous disorders then accounted for about one third of the illness experienced by people 'of condition' (the upper classes). This figure is very close to the estimates of neurotic disorders among the general population of Britain today: one person in three probably has first-hand experience of neurosis. Studies of different cultures show that both the symptoms and the incidence of neurotic disorders found in Western cities are equally typical of tribal and rural communities in Africa and Asia. So it seems that neurotic worrying is a worldwide problem which has little to do with industrialization or urban living.

Was life less stressful in the past? Arthur William Devis's Family of Anglers *contrasts vividly with the Bedlam scene from Hogarth's* The Rake's Progress.

The 'visual cliff'
demonstrates that a fear of
heights is present in very
small children. The drop is
covered by a sheet of glass,
but the baby refuses to crawl
over the glass thus showing
that he can see the depth
and hence the danger.

Anxiety – when does it start?

According to Freud, being born is a major source of anxiety. The best known exponent of this view is probably the Californian therapist Arthur Janov, whose primal therapy, outlined in his book *The Primal Scream*, is based on the assumption that many adult neuroses can be traced back to the traumas suffered at birth. However, most psychoanalysts claim that children are free from anxiety until they become old enough to appreciate the extent of their helplessness and dependence on other people. For psychoanalysts all neurotic worries have their origins in early childhood experiences. But there are two reasons for thinking this belief is false. In the first place, like other species, we seem to be born with a certain number of fears (a fear of sudden changes in height, for example) while other worries, such as fear of the dark and anxiety about strangers, develop universally at certain points in childhood, irrespective of a child's experience, and in a way that suggests that we are genetically predisposed to have fears and hence to worry. Moreover, many adult neuroses seem to stem from traumatic events experienced towards the end of adolescence or even later. And so the current view is that the importance of early experiences in determining all aspects of adult personality – including the tendency to develop neuroses – has been exaggerated.

However, anxiety plays a crucial role in socialization. It is difficult to see how children could learn to control and shape their behaviour into socially accepted patterns if they were not affected by the fear of parental disapproval or the withdrawal of love. One product of socialization is the development of a conscience, by which we experience guilt. Since many worries arise from feeling guilty, we cannot altogether ignore the past when trying to explain what is worrying us in the present.

Who worries?

The same experience makes one person worry more than another, because worrying is also a personality trait partly determined by the genes we inherit. The likelihood of someone having a neurotic breakdown is determined jointly by how prone they are to anxiety and how much stress there is in their life – it will take less life-stress to push a naturally anxious person over the top. This is underlined by the fact that people rarely suffer a neurotic breakdown for the first time late in life, although stress-inducing events may become more frequent as we get older.

The tendency to worry also varies between the sexes – women have been found to be more anxious than men, wherever the comparison has been made – and between nations, as can be seen from the table below, which was drawn up by Thomas Holmes and Richard Rahe of the University of Washington Medical School. In the course of investigating events which are generally considered stressful, they studied more than 5000 people in the USA and identified forty-three life events or changes in lifestyle that are associated with stress and disease. They then asked a larger number of people in different societies to rate the events according to the degree of readjustment entailed by each.

The table lists the fifteen events which American subjects felt required the greatest amount of readjustment, and compares this with rankings given for the same events by European and Japanese subjects. There are some interesting variations. For instance, death of a close family member ranks high for both Americans and Japanese (fifth and fourth respectively) but is way down the list for Europeans (eighteenth). Similarly, Europeans seem much less disturbed by the change of health of a family member (twentieth) than either Americans (eleventh) or Japanese (ninth), or by retirement (seventeenth, tenth, eleventh respectively) but find that pregnancy requires a major readjustment, ranking it sixth on the scale as against the Americans twelfth and the Japanese thirteenth. The reasons behind these, and other, national differences are not yet fully understood.

RATINGS FOR STRESSFUL LIFE EVENTS

Life event	American	European	Japanese
Death of spouse	1	1	1
Divorce	2	3	3
Marital separation	3	5	7
Jail term	4	2	2
Death of close family member	5	18	4
Personal injury or illness	6	8	5
Marriage	7	4	6
Being fired from job	8	9	8
Marital reconciliation	9	7	15
Retirement	10	17	11
Health change of family member	11	20	9
Pregnancy	12	6	13
Sexual difficulties	13	15	10
Addition of new family member	14	13	23
Major business readjustment	15	11	12

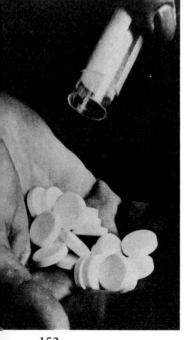

Tranquillizers such as Valium and Librium provide short-term relief from anxiety but prevent the development of the toughening up process which enables people to cope with difficult situations in the future.

Since the tendency to worry is affected by such factors as personality, sex and nationality, it is a mistake to try and apply general statements about the causes or the nature of anxiety to yourself or anyone else without taking careful account of individual characteristics. What one person finds exciting may terrify another.

ANXIETY: HOW IT AFFECTS YOU

Brain

Activity of structures in limbic system (e.g. hippocampus and amygdala) under control of long nerve-fibres starting in brainstem which act as brain's alarm system.

Body

Release of adrenalin producing:

- ☐ dry mouth
- ☐ racing pulse
- ☐ sweaty palms
- ☐ trembling hands
- ☐ pale skin
- ☐ tense muscles
- ☐ stomach contractions
- ☐ breathlessness
- ☐ tightness in chest
- ☐ dizziness

Behaviour

- ☐ aggression
- ☐ conservatism (*see* Chapter 4)
- ☐ obsessive – compulsive behaviour
- ☐ phobias

The range of anxiety

Worrying is not necessarily a bad habit: indeed, it is a perfectly normal and necessary form of vigilance. But worry can sometimes become so intense and so frequent that it becomes incapacitating, in which case it is described as neurotic anxiety. 'Normal' worry seems to involve the exercise of higher mental processes, while neurotic worry stems from more primitive centres of the brain, which may not be under voluntary control. This explains why people suffering from neurotic anxiety usually have no difficulty in recognizing that their behaviour is inappropriate but are unable to change it.

Dr Willard Gaylin, a New York psychotherapist, has a useful way of categorizing the ways in which ordinary people deal with anxiety.

□ **Seeking oral satisfaction through eating, drinking, smoking, which are forms of self-reward and reassurance**

□ **Seeking sexual satisfaction, alone or with a partner, which is a way of proving one's worth as a person**

□ **Spending money, which is a way of making oneself feel potent and lovable**

□ **Performing trivial tasks such as tidying up or cleaning, which is a way of creating a feeling of accomplishment**

These strategies can become destructive if they are taken to excess, as in alcoholism or compulsive spending or gambling, but for most people they are useful ways of coping with everyday stress.

Other common defences against anxiety are daydreaming, sleeping and taking strenuous exercise. Daydreaming is so common, in fact, that it is estimated that some of us spend 30 to 40 per cent of our waking lives daydreaming, even if most of the thoughts that cross our mind last less than fifteen seconds. Although many people are embarrassed about daydreaming, reasoning, no doubt, that it is a waste of time, the reverse is actually true. Daydreams meet a basic need for the human mind to be filled with thought, and children who daydream a lot are generally happier and more cooperative and have better concentration than those with less active imaginations.

Gambling is one strategy for dealing with anxiety but, like alcohol, it can be destructive taken to excess.

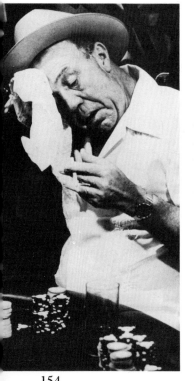

Contrary to popular belief, the old do not spend a great deal of time in reverie: daydreaming frequency decreases with age, and their thoughts are just as likely to be about the present or the future as they are about the past. There are sex differences; daydreaming is more common among women than men. At all ages daydreams are most likely to centre on solving problems, though among the young sex is also a common theme.

It is only when the everyday props such as eating, drinking, sleeping and so on fail that anxiety threatens to become a clinical problem. It is difficult to decide at what point worrying ceases to be normal and becomes neurotic. But we can safely say that it is pathological when it stops us from leading a normal existence, as with severe obsessive–compulsive disorder such as handwashing, or with phobias and anxiety-based conditions such as hypochondria.

Some phobias are highly specific, involving a fear of rats, spiders, snakes, flying or lifts, for instance. It is often possible to manage these fears fairly easily by restructuring one's life to avoid them, although spider phobics, say, may well restrict their activities because they imagine spiders lurking in the most unlikely places. Less easily dealt with are more generalized phobias, such as agoraphobia (the fear of large open spaces), claustrophobia (the fear of small, enclosed spaces), or a fear of darkness. Agoraphobia is the most prevalent problem of this kind, and is responsible for keeping millions of sufferers, most of them women, locked in their homes.

Psychological research has shown that phobias and obsessive–compulsive conditions can be seen as maladaptive conditioned response, that is to say an inappropriate form of learned behaviour. Phobics do tend to have certain definable psychological traits – they are perfectionists, achievers, extemely neat, well-groomed and with a strong sense of responsibility – but the only treatment that has had any measurable success concentrates not on their personalities, but on their behaviour, tackling the problem head on. Behaviour therapy, unlike psychoanalytic methods, has had striking success in treating these particular neurotic disorders. There are two approaches:

☐ **Flooding**

This involves confronting the patient with the feared object or situation right from the start. Being 'flooded' with emotion is particularly unpleasant, sometimes inducing feelings of panic and near suffocation, but the emotion gradually subsides and the patient begins to tolerate the situation with far greater composure. It may take twenty to thirty sessions for a phobia to be cured, but each session reduces the level of anxiety.

☐ **Desensitization**

This is the method Susan Grey used with Joan (*see* page 160). It takes a step-by-step approach, exposing the patient gradually to more and more anxiety-provoking situations.

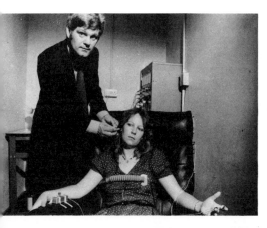

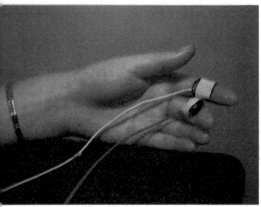

Using the polygraph to detect phobic reactions. Dr Gisli Gudjonsson is fitting a sensitive measuring device to the subject's skin, an entirely painless procedure. Electrodes on the fingers monitor the level of sweat, a flexible rubber tube round the chest measures respiration and a light-sensitive sensor on the ear lobe measures heart rate.

Suspecting that the girl has a phobia of snakes, Dr Gudjonsson reads out a list of animal names to see how she responds. He asks first if she is afraid of spiders. She says no. The pens confirm her statement. When snakes are mentioned, the subject says that she is not afraid of them either. Outwardly she looks calm, but the polygraph measures her reaction: the pens are moving wildly and indicate that she is actually close to panic. The polygraph, then, is highly efficient at recording emotional arousal although it is not able to explain why subjects may be lying.

Two polygraph techniques are used to detect deception in criminal investigations. The first compares the subject's responses to questions about a crime with responses to 'control' questions put to them in a pre-test interview. The second, known as the concealed information technique, is concerned with how people recognize certain stimuli as significant. This compares a suspect's responses to intimate information about a crime with an innocent person's responses to items that are significant in his or her life. For example, a woman's response to the carving knife from her kitchen drawer would become very different if she had used it to murder her husband!

The polygraph gives results that are better than chance, but it has its limitations. For instance, if innocent people are asked direct questions about a crime, they may register a 'guilty' reaction because they are psychologically disturbed by the questions. It should not, therefore, in Dr Gudjonsson's opinion, be used as a routine investigative tool.

Rituals and repetition

Anxiety can be seen at its most extreme in the irrational rituals of obsessive–compulsive disorders. Four main types of obsessive–compulsive behaviour have been identified by Professor S. Rachman and Dr Ray Hodgson, of the Institute of Psychiatry, London.

☐ **Obsessional cleaning**
This is characterized by excessive fear of contamination (for instance from money, public telephones or animals) and constant washing with soap and antiseptics.

☐ **Obsessional checking**
Behaviour like this can make routine activities such as brushing one's teeth or leaving the house a lengthy ritual. Checking that the gas is turned off or that doors are locked are common obsessions. The sufferer is also likely to check and recheck things mentally.

☐ **Obsessional slowness**
The sufferer is compelled to perform basic tasks such as dressing in a strict sequence which cannot be varied and turns a simple routine into a time-consuming and disruptive ritual.

☐ **Obsessional doubting and conscientiousness**
Victims of this are assailed by constant doubts about how well even the simplest tasks have been carried out, repeating them over and over again. They pay undue attention to detail and worry excessively about honesty, having a very strict conscience.

We may all exhibit these traits to a slight degree, but obsessive–compulsives are so afflicted that their particular rituals disrupt their lives and cause severe distress to themselves and their families. An obsessive–compulsive who seeks professional help will be assessed by a psychologist or psychiatrist to determine their problem and degree of difficulty.

Facing fear step by step

Phobias and compulsive rituals are time-consuming and debilitating defences against anxiety used by untold numbers of people. But they are among the conditions most amenable to treatment by psychological means.

The case of Joan offers a good illustration of how irrational anxiety can make everyday living a continual trial and the sort of professional help that a sufferer can obtain from behaviour therapy.

Joan has suffered from phobias and obsessive–compulsive neuroses for much of her life. She suffered in silence for twenty-five years before seeking help. Six years ago, clinical psychologist Susan Grey of the Institute of Psychiatry treated Joan for a glass phobia which centred on Joan's fear that splinters would get into her mouth from her hands after she touched glass. At her most anxious, Joan feared handling just about any object, glass or otherwise, and washed her hands up to sixty times a day. By the end of treatment she had conquered her anxiety and could happily pick up a glass without feeling the need to wash her hands.

The treatment made no attempt to deal with what was then a minor fear Joan had about dirt. Five years later, after a series of stressful events, this fear of dirt grew greater and became the focus of a new phobia of contamination. Joan began to have trouble touching anything that had been on the floor, handling money, or doing simple gardening without taking elaborate precautions. She decided to enlist Susan Grey's help again. *All in the Mind* went along to one of Joan's treatment sessions to see patient and therapist in action.

Like other victims of obsessive–compulsive disorder, Joan knows she is suffering from irrational anxiety and that her repeated rituals make no logical sense. But the knowledge is a source of conflict. 'I was standing with my hands in the sink, knowing that it was not necessary, but I was compelled to do it. I was fighting within myself.' There is acute embarrassment and a sense of isolation ('People don't understand. You begin to feel you're peculiar') that make it difficult for many sufferers to seek help. Daily life becomes drastically restricted. When her glass phobia was at its worst, shopping was a lengthy, painful mission: 'I'd walk miles to find a shop that hadn't a glass counter.' More recently, her fear of dirt from outdoors turned the simple task of opening a letter into a pre-ordained ritual: (pick up letter, open

159

with one hand, remove letter with other hand, keep envelope separate, wash hands before reading). Visitors were a problem; if someone sat down in a chair after having sat on the lawn, Joan would feel the need to clean the chair after their departure. Her husband was required to wash his hands after picking up a letter (it might harbour germs, having been on the floor).

The behavioural treatment Susan Grey used with Joan is more concerned with the problem behaviour than the reasons behind it (although possible causes of the problem are also discussed during the treatment session). The treatment entails a detailed analysis of that behaviour, and uses a series of graduated exercises that are tailor-made for the patient, drawing on the principles of learning theory. The treatment consists of a sequence of well-defined steps:

☐ **Evaluation**

> The therapist interviews the patient at length and makes use of a questionnaire to identify the behaviour that needs to be modified.

☐ **Anxiety hierarchy**

> A list of situations which give rise to anxiety and compulsive behaviour is drawn up, in order of ascending difficulty.

☐ **Exposure and Response Prevention**

> Patients are exposed to the stimuli which usually give rise to compulsive rituals, but are encouraged to refrain from carrying out the rituals which would 'neutralize' this exposure. The treatment usually provokes some anxiety, so the patients start with situations at the bottom of the hierarchy and work upwards in the course of treatment, at each stage allowing the anxiety to subside naturally. If the patients give in to the urge to make neutralizing responses, then the effort of the exposure exercises will have been wasted, so it is essential that patient and therapist work as a team with the patient participating fully in determining the pace of the treatment.

Once the first three steps (evaluation, drawing up the anxiety hierarchy and learning relaxation) have been completed, Joan's fear of contamination from garden soil is tackled directly in a controlled sequence of stages. As a first step, Susan Grey encourages Joan to touch herself after she has touched roses growing in the garden – she finds this not too difficult, since the roses are 'relatively clean'. Joan then pulls up weeds ('dirty, nasty'). Her next task is to handle a stone; she is able to do this and afterwards to touch her face with her hands still unwashed. She then touches her tongue with her fingers and again touches her own clothing. The next stage – touching the lawn – is a big hurdle: 'I'm trying not to cry.' Having managed this, she touches her clothes and face again, in that order, then succeeds in eating a biscuit despite her distress at having dirty hands: 'It makes my heart beat go faster, gives me palpitations, makes me tense.'

These transitions into uncharted psychological territory are made easier for Joan because Susan Grey performs each action first. Setting an example in this way – what psychologists call *modelling* – reduces Joan's anxiety. Susan Grey also includes occasional appeals to reason while demonstrating the actions to be performed: 'A normal person who's gardening would be able to pick up a stone like that, and then throw it away and just wipe the dust off.'

During the controlled exposure stage – while Joan is actually performing the dreaded acts – Susan Grey urges her to remain relaxed: 'That's all right, just relax'; 'Don't panic.' When each goal has been achieved, Joan receives positive reinforcement or praise: 'That's really

In a treatment session, Joan follows Susan Gray's example and touches the grass.

161

good'; 'Well done'; 'Excellent.' For homework, Joan is told to practise some of the things she has learned to do, such as touching the grass with her fingers and then 'contaminating' her clothes. This repetition acts as further reinforcement. Later sessions will involve even harder tasks such as sitting and rolling on the grass.

Joan herself says that although she is 'not completely better', and although the treatment was 'a bit traumatic at times', the therapy has been very valuable. She would recommend anyone suffering from a similar problem to seek professional help. But she adds that the patient must be prepared to put in a great deal of effort on his or her own account.

The successful treatment of a wide range of phobias and obsessive–compulsive disorders is a triumph of behaviour therapy and one of the great success stories of modern psychology. An estimated 90 per cent of patients like Joan can be cured or greatly helped by behaviour therapy – a strikingly high success rate in any field – though they must first be willing to ask for help. To most of us there is no great virtue in being able to open a letter or handle money without straight away washing our hands, but for Joan learning to do these simple things means the difference between a life of fear and the freedom to live.

After touching the grass, Joan then touches her face without first washing her hands. Finally, still without washing, Joan reluctantly eats a biscuit.

CAN WE CHANGE?

The fact that you are reading this book illustrates
something very important about both you and
psychology. Psychology is a *reflexive* science; those who
study it are studying themselves. Moreover,
self-analysis is one of the most characteristic human
mental activities. It includes the ability to recognize that
we are less than perfect and an understanding that other
people are different from us, as well as the imagination
to see that we ourselves might be different. Of course,
any concern with change or self-improvement varies
enormously in intensity between different people, and
even in the same person between one period of life and
another. Some people seem to be perpetually
discontented with themselves and their lot, while others
are prepared to look on the bright side and make the
most of their own personality and whatever life throws
their way. We would guess, however, that most readers
of *All in the Mind* are interested in the possibility of
self-generated change. So in this last chapter we show
what psychology can offer by way of tips and principles
for self-improvement. We shall also see what answers
psychologists give to some of the questions they are most
frequently asked about the pros and cons of change.

Is change desirable?

From a biological point of view, the human race is a system designed by evolution to change as the environment changes. That does not mean that personal change is easy. A method of coping with one situation can in fact get in the way when we need to find a method to cope with a different situation. But it does mean there is nothing unnatural about trying to change yourself.

Conservative thinkers, however, are opposed to change generally, and to self-generated personal change in particular. (Remember that conservatism was defined in Chapter 4 as anxiety in the face of uncertainty.) They claim that the drive for change is a modern aberration and almost certainly bad for us. There is some truth in this claim. Since the psychologist's definition of a stressor is anything that requires us to adapt or change ourselves, change is undeniably stressful, a point worth bearing in mind when you are preparing yourself for change (*see* Psychology in Action (1), p. 180).

It is only partly true that the urge to improve ourselves is a modern invention. Self-betterment is a theme which has run through literature since classical times, as well as playing a part in the teaching of most of the great religious thinkers. But universal education and mass culture – both comparatively recent phenomena – have certainly made us more aware of lifestyles alternative to our own. The old social order has vanished too, and with it the unquestioning acceptance of a fixed position in society. Social mobility, weakening of old class allegiances and traditional values, and the post-war economic boom have all worked together to ensure that many of us now entertain the vision of a different life and a new personality to match it. The media have played an important part, too, amplifying the trends and creating a climate in which the concept of personal change has become not just possible but necessary. Colour Supplement Man is *definitely* into self-improvement!

Do psychologists approve of change?

Considering what a strong vested interest they have in promoting the idea, psychologists have in the past been surprisingly cautious about the possibilities for personal growth or change. This is particularly true of the psychoanalysts, who argue that we are so dominated by biological instincts like sex and aggression that we have only a restricted choice about how we behave. Add to this an insistence that our personality is set for life as a result of what happens to us in early childhood, and you

The struggle with oneself. Christian battles with Apollyon in Bunyan's Pilgrim's Progress.

begin to understand the pessimism which runs through the writings of Freud and his followers.

There is another very influential school of psychology which tends to pour cold water on the notion that people might be able to change themselves. Theories of personality *traits* or *types* propose that we are born with fixed psychological predispositions that dictate the way we behave throughout our lives. The idea that we are born introverted, submissive, bad-tempered (or whatever) has considerable popular appeal, because it allows us to excuse a lot, without really having to think. We just say that *X* shouts because he is bad-tempered, or that *Y* becomes tongue-tied in front of an audience because she is shy. But of course this sort of 'explanation' does not really explain anything at all. It also ignores two very important features of the way people actually behave: we do *not* react in the same way in every situation, nor do we pass through life without experiencing quite substantial changes in our character, even if we make no conscious effort to change. We shall return to both these points later.

In recent years, sections of the psychological community have become much more ambitious in the claims they make about helping people to change themselves. We may not hear much these days about the Alternative Society which captured the public imagination at the beginning of the 1970s, but many of the theories and therapies which sprang up during the Me Decade are still very much in evidence. To pick out just a few at random, there is assertiveness training to gee you up, and meditation or relaxation exercises to calm you down; there are social skills courses to make you more agreeable, and EST if you want to become more dynamic and don't mind listening to trainers who are anything but agreeable! Then there are encounter groups to put you in touch with yourself, and if you don't like what you find there, an enormous range of therapies to help you iron out the flaws that stand between you and perfection.

If that sounds a little cynical, it is a reaction to some of the more extreme claims that have been made on behalf of one or two of these approaches to behavioural change. Unfortunately it is the failures – especially the expensive ones – that tend to get noticed. Psychology's success stories are less spectacular affairs, but none the less real for that. Most of them begin with modest, carefully defined and restricted goals; indeed, this is essential to their success. But the behaviour in question – whether it

In Biofeedback, students learn to be aware of and to regulate their brain rhythms and body functions as a means of self-improvement.

concerns a loss of weight, the ability to address an audience or an answering machine, or giving up smoking – is often so important to the person involved that this small change is accompanied by a dramatic improvement in their view of themselves.

As a result, psychologists can now definitely be said to be in favour of change, and most see their role as that of helping people to change *themselves*, rather than of being in possession of magical skills that can bring about change in others.

Isn't it all decided by our genes?

One of the arguments most frequently put forward to explain the fact that personal change can be very difficult is that we are slaves to our heredity. Many physical conditions have a large genetic component – height, life-expectancy and proneness to a wide range of illnesses – so why should the same not be true of our behaviour and personality? And if it is, what possible hope do we have of ever changing ourselves?

Like any other sort of *biological determinism*, this line of arguing appeals most to those who are more interested in excusing than in understanding themselves, and of course to those with a vested interest in maintaining the *status quo*. It is no accident that an English aristocrat was one of the founding fathers of behaviour genetics!

A number of other points must be made about the extent and the nature of genetic influences. Behaviour itself can never be inherited. Alcoholism may run in families, but it is a type of temperament rather than the act of raising glass to mouth that is passed down from one generation to the next. Nor can we ignore the significance to the young children involved in an environment in which they have frequent opportunities to observe respected and loved adults performing the motor sequence in question.

Mention of the environment brings us to one of the most important practical aspects of the nature-nurture controversy: even when we are dealing with a characteristic that is strongly influenced by genetic factors – height, for example – it is still open to us to try to control it by non-genetic means. Physical growth can be enhanced, as it can be stunted, by manipulating the environment in which it occurs. Given that genes play a much smaller role in shaping psychological attributes than physical ones, how much greater must the possibilities be for us to modify psychological growth?

It is probable – though not certain – that we are born

Sir Francis Galton (1822-1911), pioneer in genetics and the measurement of intelligence.

with nervous systems predisposed to develop along
certain lines with respect to such important aspects of
personality as intelligence, anxiety and impulsivity. But
that is a far cry from saying that any of these attributes
are inherited, let alone from claiming that there is no
point in trying to become cleverer, less shy or more
cautious. As it happens, the three examples chosen are
all instances of areas in which psychologists are quite
optimistic about helping people to change themselves.

Aren't the early years the ones that really count?

The idea that our earliest learning experiences count
for more than later ones, and that experience in infancy
has a disproportionate effect on what sort of adults we
become, has appealed to philosophers and
educationalists since the time of Plato. 'Give me the
child and I will give you the man' and 'Childhood shows
the man, as morning shows the day' are typical of the
many statements that express the same sentiment. So it
is one of the most impressive and important discoveries
of modern psychology to have established that the belief
that trauma in infancy always leaves irreversible scars is
actually false. So too is the claim that all adult neuroses
have their roots in the first years of life.

Perhaps the most dramatic illustration of this is
embodied by a pair of twins in Czechoslovakia who were
brought up in complete isolation, locked in a cupboard,
and deprived of adequate food and fresh air between the
ages of eighteen months and seven years. At this point,
their plight became known to the authorities and they
were taken into care, scarcely able to walk, terrified of
other people, and functioning intellectually at the level
of typical three-year-olds.

If there were any truth in Freud's assertion that all
adult neuroses are acquired before the age of six, let
alone in the claim made by the behaviourist J.B. Watson
that our emotional disposition is set for life by the time
we are three, they were surely beyond redemption.
What actually happened is that by the age of fourteen
the children had normal IQ scores, were deeply attached
to their foster mother, and had no difficulty in getting on
well with other children and adults. So much for the idea
that it's futile to fight against the results of early
misfortune!

The contemporary view is that although sensitive and
responsive parenting does provide a solid basis of trust
on which later intimate relationships can be built, the
absence of such treatment does not inevitably result in

167

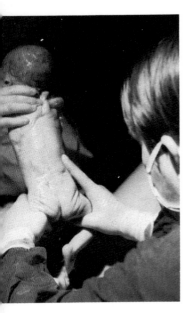

Despite inherited characteristics present from birth, the individual is ultimately responsible for his or her own behaviour.

irreparable damage. As we saw in Chapter 2, social skills and relationship training show that it is never too late to learn to love or be loved. Relationships are *easier* for those who have learned their rules at the beginning of life, but failure to do so does not rule out later learning.

It is also a myth that we are doomed as adults to remain the same sort of people we were in childhood. Children certainly have distinctive personalities from the moment they are born. These result from their genes, their experiences in the womb and during birth, and the conditions into which they are born. But researchers find that measures of what children are like before they go to school tell us very little about the sort of people they are likely to become. Even concerning intelligence, the correlation between infant and adult IQ is virtually zero. For other aspects of personality, like passivity, achievement and anger, few measures taken before the age of six show any long-term consistency. Indeed it is not until early adolescence that we can predict adult personality with any degree of confidence.

What *does* tend to remain constant, however, is the overall quality of a particular child's experiences. As a general rule – there are of course exceptions – a child who is well looked after at two will be well cared for at eight or at twelve. Similarly, the chances are that a child who is leading a deprived existence in infancy will continue to suffer throughout development. What this means is that even when we do notice a connection between a particular type of adult personality and a certain kind of upbringing, it is usually not possible to pinpoint a specific period of childhood as critical in someone's development. This has important practical implications for social policy on such matters as adoption and fostering, and it is a final nail in the coffin of the idea that the early years are the only ones that really matter.

What can we change?

Because failure tends to stick in the mind longer than success, many of us may become rather pessimistic about our ability to change ourselves. We remember the broken New Year's resolutions and the abandoned diets rather than our achievement of what may once have looked like impossibly difficult tasks – learning to ride a bicycle or to drive a car, overcoming our fear of the water or the dentist, and even managing to divorce ourselves from such lifelong partners as sugar or cigarettes. Popular mythology has built up the last of these – giving up smoking – into such an impossibly difficult task that it is perhaps worth quoting the surprising findings of a recent survey of 2700 British ex-smokers: only six per cent of them felt bad-tempered or put on weight as a result of giving up, whereas more than half of them claimed they had not found it difficult to stop!

There is actually an abundance of evidence that we can change ourselves. But we must choose the right things to alter, and set about doing so realistically. Consider weight loss, which over the years has vied with smoking as the area in which most people would like to see a change in themselves. Research shows that 97 per cent of people who go on a diet weigh as much, or more, a year later. But this does *not* mean that there is nothing to be done about surplus pounds. The first point to make is that the great majority of those who diet have no real need to be starving themselves. They are not medically overweight, but are just under the misapprehension that being thinner will automatically make them healthier or more attractive.

More important, we now know that severe dieting is an inefficient way to lose weight. The only reliable way of doing so involves a systematic and permanent change of eating habits coupled with regular exercise. The problem is one we might be able to get rid of altogether if mothers could be persuaded to be more careful about the diet of their babies in the first year of life.

It was pointed out earlier that some personal changes can take place without any conscious effort on our part. For example, parents of teenagers who get into trouble can take heart from the fact that although more than half of the British male population commits a criminal offence at least once during adolescence, only a handful continue to do so beyond their early twenties. Moreover, progress through the adult years is for most people marked not only by a modest physical decline, but by personality changes which tend to be to our advantage. Researchers have found that most of us gain in self-confidence, happiness, security and emotional stability between the ages of thirty and sixty. Although these are only general trends – individual misfortunes can of course produce a very different picture – they do make the point that psychological changes often take place without any effort on our part.

But what personal changes can we make deliberately? A complete new personality, like an overnight change, is impossible for most people. The nearest thing to it can

The possibility of change lies within all of us.

be seen in religious conversion or as the result of appalling trauma, and even these only take a really dramatic form with people of a certain kind. In fact, a total change of personality – wanting to be someone else – is something that seems to hold little appeal for adults. According to surveys, almost all of us are content with our mature personality. (The same surveys indicate that thirty is the age at which we consider our personality finally settles down.)

What most of us want to change is the face we present to the world, in the form of overt behaviour. For example, most chronically shy people say they could live with their acute self-awareness (*see* Recipes for Change (1), p. 172) if it didn't make them clam up when confronted by a stranger. In the same way, many over-anxious mothers would be happy if only their concern could be redirected towards people who were genuinely in need of care and attention. Identifying specific characteristics that are at present a source of weakness, and either neutralizing them by understanding, or turning them into strengths by redirecting them, is the sort of change we are all capable of making, with the minimum of outside assistance. Mention of understanding brings us to an important principle for change. Often *merely understanding why you do something gives you the power to control it*. Such a power in an explanation can be seen in the result of a trip to the doctor. It is a common observation that merely listening to a diagnosis and hearing a label being attached to a collection of symptoms is sufficient to relieve at least some of the distress caused by those symptoms. Understanding causes can play a vital part in changing our reactions to such debilitating states as loneliness and depression, and even an incorrect explanation may be better than none at all (*see* Psychology in Action (1), p. 180).

Can anyone change themselves?

Happily, as a general rule the greatest possibility for change lies with those who need it most. In childhood, for example, it is much easier to remedy cognitive deficits amongst children who have suffered from deprivation than it is to create superbrains. In adulthood, too, change is most likely to take place when it involves realizing untapped potential (*see* Recipes for Change (2), p. 176), getting rid of undesirable habits, or recovering from events that have harmed us.

One possible exception to this rule concerns the addictive personality. A craving – whatever its cause –

for, say, drugs that stimulate (or depress) the central nervous system is one of the most difficult habits to shake off. Psychologists who are trying to help smokers abandon their habit (*see* Psychology in Action (2), p. 182) establish as early as possible what part the stimulating effects of nicotine play in a particular smoker's dependence. 'Stimulation smokers' need to be offered alternative sources of stimulation – perhaps nicotine-flavoured chewing-gum – with the hope that a non-pharmacological stimulant like regular physical exercise may be substituted later.

Age too can be an important factor in how easy we find it to change ourselves. We have already seen that there is very little in common between the child of three and the adult he or she turns into, which shows how malleable we must be before we reach maturity. As children and as adolescents, most of us pass through periods of dissatisfaction with ourselves. We want to be cleverer, more attractive, less shy, more like someone else. Such is the plasticity of immature human beings that we actually achieve many of these ambitions. When we reach adulthood, work and family responsibilities leave us with less time for introspection, and by the end of our twenties, most of us feel that our options for changing have become much more restricted. It's not that we lose all interest in self-improvement. But the targets for change have altered. Bad habits built up over years begin to take their toll, and it is these that provide the focus for most of the adult urge to change ourselves.

Although everyone has it in them to change themselves in some way, few of us realize our full potential for change. There are many reasons for this. The first is lack of adequate motivation. It is a truism that the weak-willed find it most difficult to alter their behaviour. Other people can also be a powerful deterrent to self-generated change. The less confidence we have in ourselves and the more we rely on the approval of peers and partners, the more likely it is that our urge to change will perish in a hostile social environment. Most of us also become more set in our ways as we get older, and of course change requires not just learning but unlearning. Anything that makes us less flexible makes change less probable.

But it is never impossible. Throughout this book we have seen examples in many different areas of life where ordinary people have managed to bring about significant changes, in themselves as well as in other people. No single approach can offer a guarantee of success,

With proper support it is possible to break free from a dependency on hard drugs, despite distressing and prolonged withdrawal symptoms.

although we can say with some certainty that personal change is impossible if two conditions are not met. The first is that you need to be very clear exactly what it is about yourself that you are trying to alter. Just as important, the target for change must be a realistic one. But perhaps the single most important principle is to work on the assumption that you *are* going to change. You have to prepare yourself mentally for being a different person – however small the change you are contemplating. We may not have found a magic recipe for self-improvement, but we do at least know where to look for it. It is of course, All in the Mind.

Make the most of yourself

RECIPES FOR CHANGE 1

Being a whiz-kid may not be right for you.

The wisdom of the ancient Greeks was encapsulated in two words carved on the wall at the entrance to the Delphic Oracle. Translated, they read Know Yourself. Two and a half thousand years later, psychologists and psychiatrists offer their clients the same advice. Ignorance about yourself is *not* bliss – especially if you are seriously interested in changing yourself.

Not knowing yourself well enough is often *why* you are dissatisfied and want to change. A lack of self-knowledge can also lead you into a lifestyle totally at odds with your nature – especially where work is concerned.

We saw in Chapter 5 that being in the wrong job can be a major source of stress, and thus dangerous to your physical and mental health. Research shows that different jobs suit different personalities. So you obviously need to think about your own personality before deciding upon a career in the first instance, and later use your self-knowledge to choose between different organizations in whatever career you have chosen. It is important not to jump to the conclusion that feeling dissatisfied with a job means that there must be something wrong with you – or it. You may just be unsuited to each other. For example, a chronically shy secretary can sink without trace in a rowdy typing pool, whereas a more forthcoming one may complain of social starvation if stuck in an office by herself. But swap them round and you have two contented workers.

For practical purposes, the most important thing to find out about yourself is where you fall within the personality dimension known as introversion–extraversion, because this affects virtually every aspect of your life. The major characteristics of extreme extraverts are that they are very impulsive indeed and highly sociable, whereas extreme introverts are just the opposite. The reason for this difference probably lies in brain chemistry. An introvert's brain is naturally more active and aroused – regardless of what is going on – whereas an extravert has relatively little spontaneous activity in the nervous sytem. If we assume that there is an ideal level of activity at which the human brain functions best, then we can see why extraverts tend to seek out extra excitement – via parties, people, frequent changes of job and taking plenty of risks – while introverts behave in exactly the opposite way, doing all they can to avoid extra excitement by sticking to familiar people and situations, and wherever possible avoiding the unexpected.

No more than one person in five can really be called *an* introvert or *an* extravert. The rest of us fall somewhere between the two extremes, extraverted in some respects but introverted in others. It is perfectly possible to be a very sociable person who nevertheless plays safe in the choice of friends, as in everything else. To find out accurately where you fall in this crucial dimension of personality, you could consult the book *Know Your Own Personality*, by Hans Eysenck and Glenn Wilson. But you can get a rough idea by answering these six questions:

☐ **Do you prefer action to planning for action?**

☐ **Do you usually take the initiative in making new friends?**

☐ **Would you call yourself a lively individual?**

☐ **Would you be miserable if you were stopped from meeting lots of people?**

☐ **Are you generally quick and sure in your actions?**

☐ **Are you happiest when you're involved in a project which calls for rapid action?**

You must answer Yes or No to every question. (Just say whichever seems to be more true for you, because there are no right or wrong answers.) The more Yeses you have given, the more extraverted you are, and the more likely it is that you have a relatively low level of

The modern phenomenon of group therapy helps participants to express stifled emotions.

spontaneous activity in your nervous system, which explains why you are such a sensation-seeker and get bored so easily. Get your partner to answer the questions, but do not be surprised (or alarmed) if his or her personality turns out to be rather different from yours. Research shows that where personality is concerned, like stubbornly refuses to pair off with like. Mr Average also tends to be significantly more extraverted than Miss or Mrs Average, but that is not to say that they cannot cohabit happily. In fact, the introvert–extravert combination makes good domestic sense once you realize that introverts tend to be morning types, whereas extraverts are brighter in the evenings.

Two other aspects of personality have a crucial influence on how well we get on with other people – shyness and assertiveness. Both affect how successful we are, in private life as well as professionally. Forty per cent of us describe ourselves as shy. In adulthood, it is a condition that afflicts women more than men. There are two different sorts of shyness, however, and only one of them is a real threat to progress at work.

To find out which kind of shy person you are, see how many of the following statements you agree with:

☐ **I'm always trying to figure myself out.**

☐ **Sometimes I get the feeling I'm somewhere else, watching myself.**

☐ **I think about myself a lot.**

☐ **I'm often the subject of my own fantasies.**

Now see what you think about another list of statements:

☐ **I usually worry about making a good impression.**

☐ **I'm concerned about what other people think of me.**

☐ **One of the last things I do before leaving the house is to have a look in the mirror.**

☐ **I'm concerned about the way I present myself.**

You probably agreed with at least one statement in both lists, but if you agreed with more in the first list than in the second, you are a privately shy person. In which case your shyness should not be an obstacle to getting on at work, because the odds are you can force yourself to turn it on in public when you need to impress people, however much inner anguish it causes you. But if you agreed with more of the statements in the second list, you suffer from *public* shyness, which is more of a handicap, professionally speaking. Whereas the privately shy person worries about *feeling* bad, public shyness is the fear of *behaving* badly. So publicly shy people sit in silence at a meeting, even when they know they have an important contribution to make.

Fortunately, public shyness is not incurable. Psychiatrists run clinics for the chronically shy, and in some parts of the UK there are self-help groups run by sufferers. If all else fails, remember the first rule of getting on at work: your job has to suit you. If it doesn't, and you decide it is because of an aspect of yourself you are unwilling or unable to change, remember that not every job demands that you should be able to perform in public.

If you are interested in getting promoted, however, there is another closely related aspect of personality that is useful in virtually all professions. You need to be noticed, which means being able to assert yourself. But you must realize that assertiveness is not the same as aggression. Assertiveness involves not allowing yourself to be pushed around, insisting that your rights be respected, and making sure that your point of view is heard. Aggression involves something rather different: wanting to push other people around, often denying them their rights in the process and preventing them from expressing their opinions.

Research confirms that women are less assertive than men. But it is also well established that women can learn to become more assertive by means of assertion training, which is often provided by the same psychiatrists who run shyness clinics. If either is an aspect of yourself you are anxious to change, you could start tackling the problem by carrying out the exercises suggested in a book by the American psychologist Philip Zimbardo, *Shyness: What it is and What to do About it.*

Gregarious situations are often the most painful for the shy person.

Aggressive behaviour is usually harmful, while the results of assertion tend to be more positive.

Make the most of your brain

Artur Rubinstein, performing in concert with undiminished memory and artistry at the age of 88. Only deterioration of his sight caused him to retire from the concert platform in the following year and concentrate on two immense volumes of memoirs written without the aid of diaries. He died in 1982 aged 95.

Ironically, although we can design machines that carry out the most complex calculations in milliseconds, we understand very little about the cauliflower-shaped bundle of tissue responsible for our ingenuity. But the fact that we still do not know what happens in the brain when something is learned, or what it is about one person's brain that makes her or him cleverer than someone else, does not mean that psychology has nothing to say about the workings of the mind. Psychologists have not yet come up with a recipe for creating superbrains, but their experiments can help you make the most of the brain you have.

Take memory, for example. If you are like most people, you probably wish you could remember more than you do. The good news is, you almost certainly can! If you were asked to write down the names of all the English counties, you would probably get about two-thirds of them. And if you were asked to do exactly the same task, without advance warning, a week later, you would probably remember approximately the same number as before. But the curious thing is that the two lists would not be the same. Somewhere in your mind you probably have the names of all the counties – you'd certainly recognize their names if you saw a list of them. So the limitation in what you managed to remember on the two occasions was not so much in your memory store as in your ability to retrieve information from it.

The 'tip-of-the-tongue' phenomenon makes the same point. Next time you are in the frustrating position of almost but not quite being able to recall someone's name, write down all the alternatives that come into your mind. When you are finally reminded of the name you were after, the chances are that you'll find it has something in common with all the names you wrote down. Perhaps they'll all start with the right letter – Harris, Hetherington or Hoddle, when all the time you were after Harper. Or maybe they'll have the right number of syllables – Dawes, Neill or Wicks, when Burke was the name you wanted to remember. But you obviously haven't really *forgotten* the name, because it is influencing the words that come into your head.

There is no doubt that most of us underrate our memories. We would do a lot better if we had more confidence in them, and knew how to use them properly. You can make a start by exploiting the principles of memory discussed in Chapter 3. Remember, for example, that facts are more likely to spring to mind if you are in the same state and place as you were when you learned them. *When* you learn is important too. Some people swear they are better at learning at certain times of day, and research shows it is not just their imagination. There *is* a biological rhythm for learning, although it affects different people in different ways. For most of us, the best plan is to take in new information in the morning, and then try to consolidate it in the afternoon. Some more routine intellectual tasks, like mental arithmetic, tend to be done better in the early evening. But there are no general rules that apply to everyone, so it is important to discover your own rhythm. You can do it by attempting to learn, say, a set number of lines of poetry at different times of day, and seeing when most lines stick. Once you've done this, try to organize your life so that the time you set aside for learning coincides with the time your memory is operating most efficiently.

You should also be sensible about organizing *what* you are trying to learn. Setting out to memorize too much similar information at the same time can lead to confusion. If you are preparing for several different exams, don't spend a whole learning period on any one of them. A switch of material is more likely to help than be a hindrance, and it also enables you to exploit *primacy* and *recency* effects. These terms refer to the fact that what you learn when you first sit down, and the last thing you read before taking a break, tend to be remembered better than the material your eyes pass over in the middle of a learning session. The same applies to what you hear, which is why good lecturers make their most important points at the beginning of a talk, and then repeat them at the end.

Learning marathons are best avoided, because they do not make the best use of your mind. Breaks offer a double bonus: the time off gives your mind a chance to do some preliminary consolidation, and it also gives a memory boost to the learning that takes place on either side of it.

Remember too the vital importance of *how* you take new information on board. Just passively looking at it is no good, unless you happen to have a photographic memory. The more *active processing* you can do with new material, the better. You must take notes on it, rephrasing it in your own words as much as possible and trying immediately to place it in the context of knowledge you already have. How does it relate to other facts? What theories is it consistent with? And does it exemplify any important principles? The more of these questions you ask the first time you come across a new bit of information, the more likely it is to enter your own personal bank of readily accessible information.

There are also various tricks and memory systems, described in the advertisements as 'new and revolutionary', but in fact often based on techniques developed by public speakers more than two thousand years ago! However, modern psychological research supports their use. In essence, most of them advise you to reduce the information you need to remember to a small number of keywords – preferably not more than seven – each of which should trigger off strands of related but more detailed facts and figures. The keywords themselves can be remembered by the classical method of *loci*, in which you first memorize a sequence of locations – for example, the rooms and cupboards in your house – and then visualize each of the things you want to remember (or a memorable object related to them) sitting in each of the locations.

Public speaking from memory.

For example, a Labour politician might want to make an impression by delivering a speech without notes which consisted of an attack on the Tory defence policy, the decline of the National Health Service, and Mrs Thatcher's personality. To make sure that the stress of the occasion does not cause him to forget the order in which he has planned to deliver his broadside, he might prepare for it by imagining a cruise missile in his bedroom, an ambulance drawn up in his living room, and the Prime Minister locked up in the broom-cupboard by the front door.

This rather improbable example makes two points about artificial memory aids. The first is that they only really work if you are a *visualizer*, that is, someone who finds it easy to conjure up vivid mental pictures. It is well known that the two sides of the brain specialize in dealing with either verbal (left side) or figurative (right side) material. For some reason we do not yet understand, many of us are more skilled at dealing with one rather than the other type of material. The difference between a verbalizer and a visualizer is the difference between a Scrabble and a chess player, although the fact that some people are adept at both games makes the point that certain mental qualities (for example, competitiveness) come in handy in a wide variety of situations and are more important than specific skills.

If you are in any doubt as to whether you're a visualizer or a verbalizer, try going through the alphabet in your head, working out first how many letters contain an 'ee' sound, and then how many of them have a curve in their shape, when they are written in Roman capitals. Time how long each task takes you. You can easily work out the answer by writing out the alphabet and cross-checking the results against your mentally worked-out answer. Most people find the first task easier, but the less difference there is between the timing of the two tasks, the more likely it is that you are a visualizer.

Don't worry if you are a verbalizer. Even if your memory is worse than other people's, you can console yourself with two thoughts. The first is that having a poor memory is far less of a practical disadvantage than it used to be. Every new external memory device, from the simple shopping list to the microcomputer, makes natural memory less important. This is now recognized by teachers, who devote more time to teaching children to think *about* things, and much less to forcing them to commit to memory information they could perfectly well look up in a book. In school and college examinations, it is now commonplace to allow candidates to take in books containing formulae they were once required to memorize.

The new way of thinking about memory acknowledges the wisdom of the old saying that a great memory does not mean a great mind any more than a dictionary is a great work of literature.

Being who you want to be

In sharp contrast to the Freudian view that we are slaves to our instincts, and the behaviourist notion that our behaviour is shaped largely by events beyond our control, *personal construct psychology* suggests that we have the freedom to be who we want to be because *we have made ourselves who we are*. This radical suggestion has implications for anyone with problems that arise from the way they see themselves – for example, the fat person who wants to be thinner, the smoker who wants to lose the habit, or the stammerer who dreams of being a fluent speaker.

All in the Mind sat in on a personal construct psychology therapy session for a group of young stammerers. Dr Fay Fransella, Director of the Centre for Personal Construct Psychology in London, believes that a condition like stammering is to some extent chosen by the stammerer. When asked what it would be like to be fluent, stammerers often either dissolve into panic at the thought, or else produce a grandiose picture of themselves as exceptionally talented orators. It is a common and frustrating feature of traditional approaches to stammering that sufferers who seem to have conquered their impediment often relapse into inarticulacy under stress, which suggests that merely improving speech production – say by speech therapy – is not sufficient.

The approach used in personal construct psychology is to concentrate on the stammerer rather than his stammer. The psychologist tries to help create a fluent person rather than worrying too much about the actual fluency. Small groups of sufferers take part in role-playing exercises, imagining themselves to be totally fluent in a variety of situations – for example, being the suave host at a cocktail party, introducing the guests to each other, making jokes, and so on.

Participants role-play a social situation and later watch themselves on video at a therapy session for stammerers.

After each playlet has been improvised, the 'actors' discuss amongst themselves what it feels like to be fluent. They have to imagine what it would be like not to have the 'excuse' of a stammer to fall back on. How will it be when people do not always wait for you to finish your sentence, and are not transfixed by confusion or embarrassment? Conversations acquire a whole new significance when you are no longer too busy organizing what you're going to say next to listen properly to anyone else.

The new rules of fluent conversation are most easily mastered in easy, make-believe situations. The personal construct approach takes into account the way stammering develops in the first place. Children who have difficulty acquiring language may have inarticulacy reinforced by parents who pay more attention to their stammering than to fluent, more 'ordinary' speech patterns. Children can come to treat stammering as the most effective way of communicating with adults, even though they may speak quite fluently to other children or even animals.

Personal construct psychology therapists work alongside speech therapists when dealing with stammerers, and the combination significantly reduces the probability of relapse. With patients who want to be much thinner, the approach is to make them look ahead and prepare themselves for life without the traditional weapon of the fat person – the easy, self-deprecating jokes. Personal construct psychology argues that often dieters do not really want to lose weight. They may be worried that if they were thinner, they'd be expected to be more grown up or perhaps that they'd become the object of sexual attention they aren't ready for. Personal construct psychology therapists find that sometimes fat people make a conscious decision to remain fat, once they have come to understand why they are as they are. And of course psychologists must accept this, since their role is to assist with, not insist on, change.

Personal construct psychology sees self-change as a three-stage operation. The first stage consists of imagining what you will be like when you have changed. You must have a clear picture of the 'new you' before you start. In the second stage, you have to behave *as if you already are the person you'd like to be*. This is a role-playing exercise. In your heart of hearts you know you aren't yet the new person, but you get the feel of it by adopting the mannerisms and trappings of the new part. The third stage is arrived at when enactment is transformed into psychological fact. It is often a gradual process, a matter of losing self-consciousness and no longer asking whether this person who is refusing cigarettes or a second helping, or speaking without hesitation, can really be you.

Personal construct psychology makes the point that change is threatening. That is one reason why we find it so difficult. However successful you are in the end, the early stages of self-change are full of failures. It's safer not to try – not just because of these short-term failures,

181

but because you can never know the *ultimate* consequences of change. Imagining the new you is just that – an act of imagination. The reality may be different, and not necessarily to your taste. Add to that the threat which self-chosen change can pose to your relationships with other people – especially your most intimate relationships – and you can see that other people's expectations can be just as great a barrier to change as your own. But the great virtue of the personal construct approach is that it enables you to identify and understand the problems in advance, and make suitable preparations to overcome them if they should arise.

Giving up smoking

PSYCHOLOGY IN ACTION 2

Of all the habits that people want to change in themselves, smoking is perhaps the most widespread. Although their numbers have shrunk somewhat over the past decade and smokers are now in a minority, there are still about 17 million people in the United Kingdom who smoke cigarettes.

What's more, about two-thirds of smokers say that they would like to stop, so it appears that most of them are unwilling prisoners of the habit.

That most should want to quit is not surprising, given that the hundred thousand deaths from smoking each year represent by far the biggest preventable cause of death in our society. The puzzle is rather why so many continue to smoke and find they cannot give up.

Giving up smoking can be hard. Like Mark Twain, the average smoker is an expert at it: he has done it more times than he can remember. Research has shown that relapse following treatment is as common for smoking as it is for people who use hard drugs. The problem in the two cases is very similar, since pharmacological addiction is at least as important for smoking as it is for drug-taking, and in both cases there are also important social and psychological factors that help maintain the habit.

Most smokers do not see giving up smoking as a task for which they need professional help. It is they themselves who smoke and they who have to decide to stop, and nobody can do that for them. There is a lot of truth in this, and of course nobody can be 'cured' of smoking independently of what they themselves decide. But the process of quitting *can* be made easier by giving people some idea of what they are letting themselves in

for, by providing support and encouragement, and by helping them avoid some of the obvious pitfalls.

As with all successful psychological approaches to treatment, the emphasis is on helping people to help themselves. Clinical psychologist Martin Jarvis runs a clinic to help people stop smoking at the Addiction Research Unit in the Institute of Psychiatry, in South London. He begins the first session by establishing a new patient's smoking habits. How long has he been a smoker? How many cigarettes does he get through in a typical day? Has he ever tried to stop, and if so what did he find most difficult about giving up? Having established the basic data, and having tried to identify the smoker's particular pattern of smoking, he tries to find out what they are hoping to get out of visiting the clinic. He explains that the clinic does not offer magic remedies like hypnosis or acupuncture, because such treatments are not often effective. Instead he offers a series of different kinds of support for people attempting to give up smoking, ranging from nicotine-flavoured chewing-gum (to ease the physiological withdrawal symptoms) to organized sessions with other people who are also trying to become non-smokers. These groups consist of about ten people who meet every week to share experiences and discuss problems.

Jarvis emphasizes that at least 80 per cent of the effort involved in giving up smoking has to come from the smokers themselves. Preparation for giving up is crucial. A date must be set and plans made for avoiding situations in which a cigarette is likely to be most tempting during the vital first week.

As an extra inducement, the psychologist gives a practical demonstration of the physiological consequences of smoking a cigarette. He takes a small blood sample, and also gets the smoker to breathe into a machine which shows how much carbon monoxide is ingested with every puff on a cigarette. He explains that smoking causes red blood cells, which ought to be carrying oxygen, to carry poisonous carbon monoxide instead.

No single method for giving up smoking seems to work better than the others, but there are a number of helpful psychological aids. Just counting how many cigarettes you smoke and noting when you do so can cut consumption significantly. It focuses attention on the habit and stops 'automatic', unconscious lighting up. Anti-smoking groups and individual advice and discussion sessions are both known to improve the odds

Clinical psychologist Martin Jarvis counselling at the Addiction Research Unit. The tests used to demonstrate the carbon monoxide content in cigarette smoke.

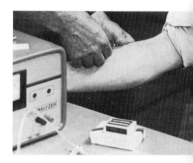

of giving up altogether. But the smokers most likely to succeed in abandoning the habit are those suffering from a serious illness directly related to smoking, which makes the point that the real key to success lies in finding sufficient leverage or incentive to provide the will-power necessary to support the change.

Checklist for change

☐ Commit yourself to the idea that change is possible.

☐ Explore your reasons for wanting to change.

☐ Check how well you know yourself.

☐ Decide exactly what it is that needs to be changed. Is it you or just some aspect of your lifestyle?

☐ Make sure you understand and are well prepared for the likely consequences of change. But you cannot be certain what they are going to be, so retain enough mental flexibility to adjust to any of a number of different post-change *personas*.

☐ Make your resolutions about change specific.

☐ Set yourself a series of modest, short-term goals rather than going for the jackpot from the very beginning.

☐ Make sure the change is something you can start on now. The *mañana* spirit is the opposite of that necessary for successful self-generated change.

☐ Avoid negative thinking. Don't assume the worst about other people's response to what you're trying to do, and don't make too much of temporary setbacks. Don't talk yourself into failure, and avoid both unrealistic strategies and people who are unlikely to help you succeed.

☐ Keep a constant check on how well you are doing. Reward yourself for successes, either by allowing yourself an indulgence, or – better – by simple self-congratulation.

☐ Beware the addictive power of self-generated change! The more difficult the process, the more rewarding its successful conclusion. So make sure you give yourself – and other people – plenty of time to enjoy each new achievement before you decide on the next target for change.

Acknowledgements

We would like to make special acknowledgement of the role of Alice Harper in shaping much of the content of this book. As researcher for the TV series she had considerable influence on the style and direction of each programme as well as carrying out much of the preliminary vetting of participants and topics. The success of her search for authoritative and relevant material is directly reflected in these chapters. We should also like to thank the Associate Editors, Janet Law and Susana Raby, who undertook the enormous and painstaking task of compiling the book from the programme scripts and contributors' essays.

Chapter 1 What is psychology?

This chapter is by Martin Lucas. It draws heavily on material supplied by Dr Andrew Colman, Lecturer in Psychology at Leicester University and author of the book *What is Psychology?*

Chapter 2 Man the social animal

The introductory material is by John Nicholson; 'Learning to Understand the Social World' was contributed by Dr Steve Duck, Senior Lecturer in Psychology at Lancaster University; 'Children's Friendships' is based on material supplied by Steve Duck; the interview with Professor Robert Hinde FRS, Director of the Sub-Department of Animal Behaviour, Cambridge University, was conducted by John Nicholson; 'Life Skills' is based on the work of Dougal Mackay, Principal Clinical Psychologist at the Barrow Hospital, Bristol; 'Friends for Life' is based on the work of Dr Michael Argyle, Reader in Social Psychology at Oxford University; 'Psychology in Action' is based on a marital therapy session specially conducted for *All in the Mind* by Dougal Mackay; 'Marriage – What Makes and Breaks It' is based on the work of Michael Argyle and Dr Adrian Furnham, Lecturer in Psychology at University College, London; 'Teach Yourself You (Finding an Ideal Mate)' is based on the test given to the *All in the Mind* studio audience and devised by Dougal Mackay.

Chapter 3 Man the thinking animal

The introductory material is by John Nicholson; the interview with Dr George Butterworth, Lecturer in Psychology at Southampton University, was conducted by Martin Lucas; 'Learning is Active' was contributed by Dr Guy Claxton, Lecturer in Psychology at the Centre for Science Education, Chelsea College, London University; 'Increase Your Memory Power' is based on the work of Dr Alan Baddeley, Director of the British Medical Research Council's Applied Psychology Unit, Cambridge University; 'Teach Yourself You (Questions of Memory)' is adapted from the test given to the *All in the Mind* studio audience and a discussion with Dr Michael Howe, Senior Lecturer in Psychology at Exeter University; 'Memory and Ageing' is based on the research of Professor Patrick Rabbitt of Manchester University; the experiment on the conservation of volume was conducted by Maggie Mills, Honorary Lecturer in Psychology at Bedford College, London University; the experiment on the effects of alcohol on learning was carried out on students at Bedford College by Alice Harper, of Thames TV.

Chapter 4 Attitudes, beliefs and prejudices

The introductory material is by John Nicholson; 'The Roots of Prejudice' is based on material supplied by Professor J. Richard Eiser, of the Psychology Department, Exeter University; 'Teach Yourself You (How Prejudiced Are You?)' is based on the test given to the *All in the Mind* studio audience; the interviews with Dr Raymond Cochrane and Dr Michael Billig, of Birmingham University Psychology Department, were conducted by John Nicholson; 'Psychology in Action' is based on a film made for *All in the Mind* at Farnham Castle, home of the International Briefing Centre, and an interview with Peter Aylett, the course organizer. The experiment on how prejudice operates in daily life was conducted by Dr Mary Sissons, of the Department of Social Psychology, Sussex University.

Chapter 5 Work: do we need it?

The introductory material is by John Nicholson; 'Support in the Workplace' is based on material supplied by Professor Cary Cooper, of the Department of Management Sciences, UMIST; 'Work-related Stress' is based on the work of Cary Cooper and Michael Argyle; 'The Danger of Cognitive Overload' is based on interviews with Dr Donald Broadbent FRS, former Director of the MRC Applied Psychology Unit, Cambridge, and Wing Commander C.C. Rustin, Officer Commanding Handling Squadrons, Boscombe Down Aeroplane and Armaments Experimental Establishment, conducted by John Nicholson and Alice Harper; 'Teach Yourself You (The Instant Stress Detector)' was adapted by Cary Cooper from a much longer questionnaire especially for the *All in the Mind* studio audience; the interview with Professor Peter Warr, Director of the Social and Applied Psychology Unit at Sheffield University, was conducted by John Nicholson; 'Psychology in Action' is adapted from a film made for *All in the Mind* at Systime Computers Ltd, Leeds, and from an interview with Stephen Williams, Systime's Personnel Manager, conducted by John Nicholson.

Chapter 6 Crime and punishment

The introductory essay is contributed by Ray Bull, Senior Lecturer in Psychology at the North East London Polytechnic and Alice Harper; 'We Have Ways . . .' is based on material supplied by Barrie Irving, of the Police Foundation, London, and Dr Gisli Gudjonnson, Lecturer in Psychology at the Institute of Psychiatry, London; 'Teach Yourself You (Fit the Face to the Crime)' is based on the test given to the *All in the Mind* studio audience and adapted from a large-scale study carried out by Ray Bull; the interviews with Dr Ron Clarke, Director of the Home Office Research and Planning Unit, and Tony Black, Head of the Psychology Department at Broadmoor Hospital, were conducted by John Nicholson; 'Psychology in Action' is adapted from a film made for *All in the Mind* at Redlees Intermediate Treatment Centre, Isleworth, and interviews with Margery Rooke, project leader at Redlees, and Professor Norman Tutt, of the Applied Social Studies Department, Lancaster University, conducted by John Nicholson; 'True or False?' is based on material supplied by John Nicholson.

Chapter 7 Anxiety

The introductory treatment is by John Nicholson; 'Anxiety, Reward and Punishment' is based on material supplied by Professor Jeffrey Gray, head of the Department of Psychology at the Institute of Psychiatry, London; the interview with Jeffrey Gray was conducted by John Nicholson; 'Worrying' is adapted from *Habits* by John Nicholson, *Selfwatching* by Ray Hodgson and Peter Miller, and *The New York Times Guide to Personal Health* by Jane Brody; 'Rituals and Repetition' is adapted from *Selfwatching* by Ray Hodgson and Peter Miller; 'Psychology in Action' is adapted from a film made for *All in the Mind* of a therapy session conducted by Susan Grey of the Institute of Psychiatry, London. The polygraph was demonstrated by Dr Gisli Gudjonsson.

Chapter 8 Can we change?

This chapter is written by John Nicholson. It incorporates information and suggestions provided by Dr Don Bannister, of High Royds Hospital, West Yorkshire; Dr Donald Broadbent FRS, of the Department of Experimental Psychology, Oxford University; Professor Alan Clarke, of the Psychology Department, Hull University; Dr Fay Fransella, of the Centre for Personal Construct Psychology, London; Dr Jeffrey Gray, Professor of Psychology at the Institute of Psychiatry, London; Dr Martin Jarvis, of the Addiction Research Unit, at the Institute of Psychiatry, London; Dougal Mackay, Principal Clinical Psychologist at the Barrow Hospital, Bristol; and Alice Harper and Martin Lucas.

Bibliography

Baddeley, A. (1983). *Your Memory, A User's Guide.* Penguin Books, Harmondsworth.

Bannister, D. and Fransella, F. (1971). *Inquiring Man.* Penguin Books, Harmondsworth.

Bull, R., Bustin, B., Evans, P. and Gahagan, D. (1983). *Psychology for Police Officers.* John Wiley, London.

Clarke, A.M. and Clarke, A.D.B. (1976). *Early Experience: Myth and Evidence.* Open Books, London.

Colman, A. (1981). *What is Psychology?* Kogan Page, London.

Cooper, C. (1981). *The Stress Check.* Prentice Hall, Englewood Cliffs, New Jersey.

Cooper, C. and Marshall, J. (1978). *Understanding Executive Stress.* Macmillan, London.

Donaldson, M. (1978). *Children's Minds.* Fontana Paperbacks, London.

Duck, S. (1983). *Friends for Life: The Psychology of Close Relationships.* Harvester, Brighton.

Eysenck, H.J. and Wilson, G. (1976). *Know Your Own Personality.* Penguin Books, Harmondsworth.

Hodgson, R. and Miller, P. (1982). *Selfwatching.* Century, London.

Hough, M. and Mayhew, P. (1983). *The British Crime Survey.* Her Majesty's Stationery Office, London.

Howe, M.J.A. (1983). *Introduction to the Psychology of Memory.* Harper & Row, New York.

Nicholson, J.N. (1978). *Habits: Why You Do What You Do.* Pan Books, London.

Nicholson, J.N. (1980). *Seven Ages: The Truth About Life Crises.* Fontana Paperbacks, London.

Nicholson, J.N. (1984). *Men and Women: How Different Are They?* Oxford University Press, Oxford.

Warr, P. and Wall, T. (1975). *Work and Well-Being.* Penguin Books, Harmondsworth.

Zimbardo, P.G. (1981). *Shyness: What It Is and What To Do About It.* Pan Books, London.

Index

Picture and text acknowledgements

Archives of the History of American Psychology 16
Audio Ltd 165 **Clive Barda Studios** 176 **Santo
Basone** 81, 118 **Tony Black** 131 bottom left, 134
Bridgeman Art Library 149 bottom **Ray Bull** 129,
130 **Dr. R. G. V. Clarke** 131 top left **Dr. Raymond
Cochrane** 86 **Control Data** 98 **Daily Telegraph
Colour Library** 80 **Philip Daly** 11, 18, 21, 34
Dominic Photography Catherine Ashmore 127 **Mary
Evans Picture Library** 164 **John Glover** 45 top
Guinness Superlatives Limited 66 top **Prof. Robert
Hinde** 40 **Michael Holford** 82 top **Kobal Collection**
14, 94 **Martin Lucas** 8 top **Mansell Collection** 54
Penny Millar 22, 23, 36, 41 **Multimedia** 7, 8 bottom,
27, 31, 33, 44 top, 45 centre right & bottom, 88, 100,
168, 175 bottom, Santo Basone 180, Geoff Howard 56,
57, 79, 106, 124, 125, 128, Herbie Knott 38, 39,
59–61, 71–73, 90–93, 115, 116, 138–141, 144–146,
148, 161, 162, 182, 183, John Sculpher 69, Homer
Sykes 157 **National Portrait Gallery, London** 166
Popperfoto 24 **Rex Features** 6 top & bottom right,
25, 28–30, 32, 37, 48, 66 bottom, 68, 83, 103, 108 top,
112, 123 right, 131 top centre & bottom centre, 152,
155, 171, 174, 175 top, 178 **Ann Ronan Picture
Library** 149 top **Wing Comm. Clive Rustin** 108
bottom **Mike Salisbury** 19 **Science Photo Library**
Jerry Mason 10, NASA 17 **Frank Spooner Pictures**
Gamma 84, 104, 120, 121, 123 left, 147, 169 top **Tate
Gallery, London** 9 **Thames Television** 53, 67 **Prof.
Norman Tutt** 137 **William Vandivert Assoc.** © Jim
Carr 150 **Vision International** 43, 44 centre right &
bottom, 49, 55, 63 bottom, 81 top right, centre right &
bottom right, 89, 101 top & bottom left, 111, 153, 169
bottom, Explorer 6 bottom left, 101 bottom right, 172,
Fiore/Explorer 82 bottom, Scala 76, 82 centre, 143
Volvo 97 **Peter Warr** 110 **Weidenfeld & Nicholson**,
from Eye and Brain by R. L. Gregory 63 top **Janine
Wiedel** 35, 58, 62, 65, 113, 163

Text acknowledgement
The table on page 152 is reprinted with permission
from the *Journal of Psychosomatic Research*, **vol. 11**,
Holmes and Rahe, copyright 1967, Pergamon Press Ltd.